CFI!
THE BOOK

by
Alex Stone

AWS Books
Highland, IN

Alex Stone

AWS BOOKS, December 2018
Copyright © 2018 by Alexander W. Stone

All rights reserved.
Published in the United States by AWS Books, Highland, IN

This is a work of fiction. All names, characters, businesses, products, places, and incidents either are the product of the author's imagination or are used fictitiously. Any resemblance to actual persons, living or dead, events, or locales is entirely coincidental.

This book is sold subject to the condition that it shall not, by way of trade or otherwise, be reproduced, stored in a retrieval system, be lent, resold, hired out, or otherwise circulated or transmitted without the author's prior consent in any form of binding or cover other than that in which it is first published and without a similar condition, including this condition, being imposed on the subsequent purchaser.

ISBN 13: 978-1790668793
cannondle@aol.com
www.cfithebook.com

Printed in the United States of America

CFI! The Book

This book is dedicated to anyone who ever had to ditch a 152 in a Kroger parking lot, clean puke off the instrument panel, live in their car, or "sign their life away" by endorsing a student for their first solo, all in the quest to rack up hours so you could get a real job.

Alex Stone

CFI (Certified Flight Instructor)

1. A career or part-time job that involves watching the Hobbs meter tick while spending unusual, long, and demanding hours in the cheapest, most stripped down, mechanically unsound aluminum can all for the goal of displaying the magic of rote learning to a student. Sometimes the aluminum can is known as being "airworthy," but that is a made-up word the mechanics will use to comply with the legal mumbo jumbo and is hardly ever true. The majority of the instruction is given in the busiest airspace with little to no safe-guarding, such as reliable radios, transponders, or even the most basic necessity-transparencies you can actually see out of. The students, the prime income of a flight instructor, are stubborn, top-gun wanna-be pilots who no matter how ever you try to persuade differently about the aircraft's only having one 100HP engine, will still rotate the nose to fifty degrees on takeoff—that is, if they even bother to show up for the lesson from being too (insert bullshit excuse here).

2. A brave and astute individual, most likely also an alcoholic, who tries to be killed many times on a daily basis only to be paid minimum wage if they are lucky, training cocky big-headed students who one day will have hundreds of lives in their hands.

– UrbanDictionary.com

Alex Stone

CFI! The Book

Contents

Introduction... 11

The Obligatory Right Rudder Joke... 13

1. Situational Awareness... 15

2. No Inglese... 25

3. The 92' Camry... 32

4. The King James Checklist... 38

5. Airworthiness and Registration Please... 45

6. Simulated Engine Failure... 52

7. The Instructor of the Month vs. The Prince of El Salvador 64

8. Warm Gasoline... 74

9. A Day at the Beach... 88

10. The Real Maverick... 102

11. Biennial Flight Review... 109

12. Discovery Flight... 116

13. Worst Nightmare... 125

14. First Solo... 135

15. One Thousand Hours... 145

About the Author... 149

Glossary of Aviation Terms... 150

Alex Stone

CFI!
THE BOOK

Alex Stone

Introduction

In case you didn't already know, a CFI is a certified flight instructor. Flight instruction is the most popular way for young commercial pilots fresh out of school to build flight time, and for most of us pilots it was our first paying job in the industry. Just about every airline pilot out there at one time early in their career was a flight instructor.

Typically, when a pilot finishes school and earns their commercial certificate, they have around three hundred-or-so hours of flight time. The problem is that most airlines won't give them the time of day till they have at least around a thousand. So, they have to find a way to get to a thousand.

Building time is something that every pilot starting their career has to do. People call it "earning your stripes." Flight schools pay instructors next to nothing and get away with it because they know the flight time is what their instructors really need. It's a great business for the flight school owners who are charging the students through the roof and paying the instructors by letting them lick a salt block at the end of the day for nourishment. But we put up with it, all with the hopes of a higher-paying real job at an airline later down the line.

Alex Stone

As a flight instructor, I found that most student pilots have no business being in or anywhere near an airplane. It's just not for everyone, and the number who actually complete flight school is a very small percentage of those who start. Not all of my students were bad, though. There were a few good ones that showed up on time, read the materials they were assigned, and were teachable. Those good ones made the job both rewarding and enjoyable. The first time I ever sent one of my students' solo was one of the most exciting days in my career as a pilot. To take someone who had never flown before, teach them to operate an airplane safely, and send them on their way made it all worthwhile. It was almost as exciting for me as the day I made my own first solo flight.

And seeing them progress to becoming private pilots and later commercial pilots was equally rewarding. Those good students eventually went on to be instructors themselves and later airline pilots. But this story isn't about them; it's about the other ones, the ones who had no business in an airplane. Or the ones who really didn't care to be there. They just needed something to do, so they picked this to keep their parents off their backs for a while. They're the ones who really made the job exciting, the ones who tried to kill me.

The following is a fictional story about the fictional students of a fictional flight school that's loosely based on my real experience as a flight instructor, or maybe I made it all up, or maybe it all happened exactly as written, depends who's asking. If the FAA asks, I made this all up.

The Obligatory Right Rudder Joke

You would think a funny book about flight instructing would be filled with jokes about students not using enough right rudder. Well, it's not. There's only this one:

MORE RIGHT RUDDER, MORE RIGHT RUDDER,

Alex Stone

MORE RIGHT RUDDER, MORE RIGHT RUDDER.

That should be enough. I won't mention it again.

-1-
Situational Awareness

"HOLY SHIT! What are you doing?" I screamed as I yanked back on the controls to keep the nose of the single-engine Piper Warrior from slamming into the runway. The nose had pitched down violently after my student decided to dump the flaps about ten feet above the ground, mid-bounce, during a botched landing.

"I was retracting the flaps so we could take off again," my student sitting in the left seat next to me responded. He was obviously very confused by the situation. "I thought we were doing a touch and go?"

"We were doing a touch and go, but we didn't land yet!" I'm screaming everything at this point. This wasn't the first time today that my student had tried to kill me, and it was only 8:45 in the morning. "You've got to land first! Then retract the flaps! What the hell were you thinking?"

"I thought we did land."

"No, we didn't land! We hit the runway and bounced! We were airborne again when you dumped the flaps and let the nose pitch forward!"

"Oh, sorry."

"Sorry? Man, you've got to pay attention; you're going to kill us. I'm surprised the plane is still in one piece."

"Sorry," he apologized again, as I brought the plane to a stop on the runway.

There's an old joke amongst pilots that says: "A good landing is one that you can walk away from, and a great landing is one were the airplane can be reused again afterwards." This plane still seemed reusable, I thought. *I suppose it was a great landing?*

This was how most of my days went. I was a flight instructor, which meant I sat in the right seat of a small training aircraft all day while my students tried to kill me. I had to let them take us all the way to the edge of doom—so they could learn.

My job was to save the day at the last second before they destroyed the airplane or worse, killed us both. It was hours of boredom followed by seconds of sheer terror, followed by several minutes of screaming, and then we did it again, over and over—until they learned.

I worked for a small flight school in Marbella, Florida called Marbella Flight Academy. We specialized in training the worst students out there. Got rejected from every other flight school in the country? Come on down to Marbella. We'd train you, as long as you could pay. It was our only requirement.

I moved down here for this job on the promise of 100+ hours of flying a month, and they had been delivering on that. I was flying my ass off down there and building hours. But at what cost?

Fresh out of college, building hours is the most important thing for a pilot that's beginning their career. I was getting close to having enough flight time to get a real job with an airline. I just hoped I survived till then.

One thousand hours was the magic mark all of us instructors were aiming for. I was at 632 now, hopefully 632.4 by the end of this flight. Ask any instructor how many hours they have, and they can tell you down to the tenth. The highlight of my day was when I got home and totaled up my logbook for the day. Each day getting closer and closer to having enough flight time so that I wouldn't have to do this anymore.

This guy I was "teaching" on this particular day, his name was George. George did things without thinking, such as retracting flaps mid-bounce during a botched landing. He didn't even know we had bounced; he thought we had landed. A lack of situational awareness: that's what we called it when a student was unaware of their surroundings. George was a poster child for a complete lack of situational awareness. He had no clue where we were or what we were doing right now or ever. And bouncing the landing, that's just bad stick skills. The best part was that George's horrible stick skills and non-existent situational awareness were nothing compared to his piss-poor navigation skills.

We were at a podunk little airport in Florida called Calusa, just fifteen miles northeast from our home base of Marbella, and I guarantee George cannot find his way home from here. That would have been OK if George were a new student, but he wasn't. George had 400 hours of flight instruction under his belt, and a good chunk of that time, like most of it, had been spent flying in-between these two airports.

George had more flight time than most people do when they earn their commercial certificate. In fact, he had more time than some of the instructors who had attempted to teach him. Shit, I had less flight time than he did when I first became a flight instructor, and yet George still hadn't made his first solo flight. Why? Because he couldn't land, he couldn't navigate, and he couldn't communicate with air traffic control.

Every instructor at this school had attempted to teach George. He just kept getting passed on from one instructor to another as we all became fed up with him. I was fed up, but it was my turn. And when we got these types of students, everyone had to take their turn. George was just not cut out for aviation. You wouldn't have known it by looking at him, though; he wore the *Top Gun* Ray Ban Aviators and walked around in the Florida summer heat wearing a brown leather bomber jacket. He looked the part, he wanted to be a pilot, and he wouldn't admit to himself that this was just not for him.

To make matters worse, my boss Todd, the owner of the flight school, was encouraging George to keep taking lessons. "You'll get there," Todd kept encouraging him. "Any day now we're going to send you solo."

What a bunch of crap. Todd loved George because he was cleaning him out of all his money. As long as George kept trying, Todd kept making money off him. So, George was still trying to be a pilot, and I had to keep flying with him. And I was pretty sure that any day now, he was gonna kill me.

"Well, you think you can get us home from here?" I asked him.

"Sure," he said.

"Alright, take me home," I said, knowing damn well that George would get lost again, like he did every day.

We still had forty-five minutes left in our flight slot, and it should only have taken ten minutes to get back to Marbella, but not for George. We needed to start heading back early to give him plenty of time to fly in circles while he looked for the airport.

George opened up the throttle, and we began our take-off roll. I assumed my ready position with my hands just behind the controls. I had to be ready to grab the yoke and take over when he lost control of the plane, which would, without a doubt happen again.

The nose wheel shimmied as the dilapidated 1960s single-engine Piper accelerated down the runway. This old plane was definitely showing its age after years of use as a trainer. There's no telling how many students have slammed it into the runway during near-crash landings. On the surface this jalopy of an airplane looked beaten and battered. Underneath, the airframe was probably littered with hairline cracks, all just waiting for the right jolt to come along and finish this thing off. Training aircraft are treated worse than rental cars; never, ever, buy a used one.

"So which way to Marbella?" I asked once we were airborne and climbing. All 160 horsepower of the old Lycoming horizontally opposed four cylinder struggling to give us a 300-foot-per-minute rate of climb.

"Ah, let me take a look at the chart," George responded. He began fumbling around with his VFR sectional in his lap, barely maintaining control of the plane in the process.

It was a clear day, and looking over my shoulder I could easily see the Marbella Airport behind us as we headed away from it.

"I think we should go that way." George said as he pointed north-east in the opposite direction of the airport.

"What direction is 'that way'?" I asked.

"Ah, south and west," he responded, sounding very unsure of his answer.

"That's not southwest," I said. "Look at your heading indicator."

He looked down at the instrument panel then up to the magnetic compass bouncing around on the glareshield and back and forth several times, probably trying to remember if he'd ever even set his heading indicator before we took off. "Oh yeah, well, then we should go . . . north?"

"Remember the top of the chart is north."

"Oh yeah, so should we go the other way?"

"Well," I said while pointing at his chart, "if we are here, and we want to go here, and this is north, which way do you think we should go?"

"Southwest?"

"Yup."

"Should I turn?"

"By all means, please."

George struggled to maintain a constant altitude as he turned the plane around. His altitude control was plus or minus 300 feet, at best. Riding along while he was at the controls was not for the weak stomached.

When George completed his turn, Marbella Airport was right in front of us, in plain view. "Are we going the right way?" I asked.

"I don't know. Are we?" he questioned.

"I'm asking you. Do you think we're going the right way?"

"I think so," he said as his eyes darted from his chart to out the window in a frantic effort to figure out where he was. He would point at random things on the chart, then stare out the window looking for them for a minute. Never finding what he was looking for, his eyes would return to the chart where he would pick out a new landmark to look for. But the landmarks he was pointing to on the chart were nowhere near our current position. He pointed to a lake that was near Tampa and began searching for it out the window. Then staring back at his chart, he mumbled something to himself about railroad tracks.

"Here," I said, as I grabbed his chart and drew two circles on it, then handed it back to him. "This is where we are, and this is where we are going."

The plane descended a few hundred feet while George buried his head in his lap, studying the chart. When he looked up and saw the plane diving, he pulled back abruptly, to get back to the altitude he was supposed to be maintaining. This repeated over and over; every time George looked down, he let the nose drop, and every time he looked up, he would jerk the controls back in a panic, pulling the plane into a climb. But he never made it back to the altitude that he was supposed to be holding; he just attempted to hold a new lower altitude each time. Every once in a while, he'd glance at me out of the corner of his eye to see if I'd noticed that we were now a few hundred feet lower than we were before.

"I'll give you a hint," I said, while pointing out the window directly at the airport. "Marbella is on the shoreline, straight ahead. Do you see it?"

"Ah, I'm looking for it." He squinted into the distance.

"Let me know when you see it," I said as we got closer and closer. The airport was clearly right in front of us. We went through this every single day. I could aim the nose of the plane right at the runway and point at it, and he still wouldn't see it. Hundreds of hours have been spent trying to teach George to navigate; it was hopeless.

As we flew right over the Marbella Airport, I put my head against the window, looking straight down at the runways below us. "See it yet?" I asked.

He continued to stare out the front windscreen, into the distance. "No," he said. "I think it's farther south."

"It's not farther south," I said with my head still pressed against the window. I could see a couple other planes in the traffic pattern below us.

When we crossed the shoreline and started heading out over the Gulf of Mexico I asked George if we were still heading the right way. "Should be right in front of us," he responded.

There was nothing in front of us except open ocean.

"Really?" I questioned. "Looks like we're heading out to sea."

"Oh yeah. Maybe we missed it."

"We definitely missed it," I said. "We flew right over it a few minutes ago."

"We did?" He sounded surprised.

"Yes, we did. Turn to a zero-six-zero heading, and the airport will be right in front of you."

But George didn't turn to the heading I had suggested. He started to but became distracted again, looking at his chart, and quit turning halfway. The airport passed off our left side as he flew southeast for a while, toward the Everglades.

At this point, we were running out of time. I had to be back at the flight school soon for my next student. "Turn north," I told him.

"OK," he said, "in a minute. I think I see the airport."

"No really, turn north. That's where the airport is. We're running out of time."

I took the controls, banking hard left in frustration, and pointed the plane straight at the airport. "It's ten miles straight ahead. I'm gonna call the tower. Descend down to pattern altitude, and let me know when you see the runway."

"OK," George said as he pulled the power back and began descending.

As we got closer and closer, I helped George point the plane right at the runway every time he kept veering off course. Without my help we'd probably just fly right over the airport again. About one mile from the end of the runway, George finally said, "I see it!"

Moments later, we impacted the runway.

-2-

No Inglese

When I got back into the flight school, Todd called all of the instructors into his office. "We've got a new group of students who just arrived today," he announced. "They're from Europe, and they will be staying in town for a few months to train here."

This wasn't out of the ordinary; students from Europe came to the US all the time to learn to fly. The cost of flight training in Europe was ridiculously expensive. It was cheaper for people to come and stay here in the US to get their certificates. Todd preyed on this. Since most of these students came from so far away, it's not like they could have stopped in and checked out the place and planes before they signed up. Many would have chosen somewhere else to go if they had.

The website for the flight school was the only impression of what it was going to be like here that most of these people had seen before arriving, and it was the one thing Todd actually put some effort into. The pictures on it, of course, were stock photos of new airplanes, not pictures of our actual planes. Anyone who had the option of going somewhere else to train would usually leave immediately upon arriving here and seeing what this place was really like. Todd had found a solution for that, though: they had to make a $10,000 nonrefundable deposit upfront. So, at least he was going to get that much out of them before they went elsewhere.

Todd informed us that our new students were waiting out in the lobby and handed us each folders with their info. My new student was from Italy; his name was Antonio. I headed out to the lobby to find him.

Antonio was dressed like a member of U2, black leather head-to-toe with blue-tinted sunglasses, and it was 90 degrees out. *Bono?* I thought.

After attempting to speak with him for a few minutes, it was obvious that he barely spoke a word of English. I don't speak Italian, and even if I did, he still needed to speak English to fly. I'm not an English teacher. I'm a flight instructor. This was going to be a problem.

English is the official language of aviation worldwide. No matter what country you're in, pilots and air traffic controllers must speak English on the radios. Pilots are supposed to speak only English in the cockpit as well. But in other counties when no one is looking, there are a lot who don't. Students are supposed to be able to read, write, and speak English prior to coming here to learn to fly, but Todd didn't care. He would take any student who was willing to pay. Antonio was paying and probably thought that he was getting away with learning to fly without having to learn English.

Many of the students we got there seemed like they really had no interest in learning to fly. It's like they came from rich families and their parents were pushing them to do something. So, they chose this because they saw it as a vacation in Florida.

After several frustrating minutes of trying to communicate with Antonio, I told him. "Wait here a minute. I need to go talk to Todd. I'll be right back"

But Antonio just stared at me confused. I tried to think of the Italian words for what I wanted to say. *What am I thinking? I don't know any Italian.*

"Wait right here," I said again, this time louder. As if he'd understand me if I spoke louder.

I headed back to have a chat with Todd.

Todd's office was a mess of paperwork. There were stacks of insurance forms covering his desk and papers that looked like warnings about severely past due bills scotch taped to the walls all over the room, each one with a date scribbled on it in marker, which I could only assume was the date he was expecting repossession of one of the planes or the building to be put up at the tax sale. When I walked in, he was feeding documents into a paper shredder as fast as the machine would take them. The room smelled like an overheating electric motor. He jumped in his chair when he saw me like he had been caught red handed.

"Oh, it's you," he said. Then ferociously fed the stack of papers in his hand into the machine as if he thought I was about to grab them from him and read them. The motor in the paper shredder strained under the heavy load. Then he fumbled around nervously, eyes darting around his desk till he spotted what he was looking for and grabbed another stack of papers and dropped them on the ground near his feet where I couldn't see them.

"What can I do for you?" he asked.

Todd's history was somewhat shrouded in mystery. There were several rumors that floated around between the instructors regarding his past. He was a pilot, we all knew that, but despite owning a flight school and several airplanes, he never seemed to want to fly. Some claimed that Todd used to be an instructor but quit flying after an embarrassing accident in which he ditched an airplane in a field because he had run out of gas. But as it turned out there was still plenty of fuel in the plane, he just had forgotten to switch the fuel selector. They say he lost his license as a result of it. Some say he *was* the instructor who taught the 9/11 terrorists and had received some sort of hush money from the government in exchange for not talking to the media. The rumor was that he used the money to open this flight school. Another rumor claimed Todd was once an airline captain but was fired after slapping a female first officer because she missed a radio call.

I never really knew which story to believe; they all seemed like possible candidates for the truth. Maybe they were all true, but I was leaning toward the latter. The guy ran this place like a merciless tyrant, and it wouldn't surprise me a bit if he'd slapped around an FO or two in his day.

I told him that I couldn't fly with Antonio.

"What's the problem?" Todd asked. "He paid upfront."

"It's not about the money. He doesn't speak English. How am I supposed to teach him to fly if he doesn't understand what I'm saying?"

"Well, he signed the form saying that he was able to read, speak, and write English," Todd stated matter-of-factly, like no one had ever lied about this before.

"He probably couldn't read the form and didn't know what he was signing."

"Well, he signed the form, so I'm sure he could read it."

"This is one hell of a screening process we've got here."

"Hey, he's a paying customer. I already cashed his check, and I'm not refunding it, so do what you can. You need the flight time, don't you?" He paused. "What do you care if he doesn't learn to fly? I mean, I'm not saying you have to actually teach him anything, just fly around with him till his money runs out, and then he'll go home just like the rest."

This was Todd's ideal situation. Run the students broke and then send them home with nothing to show for it except an empty bank account. Then he hoped they would find a way to come up with more money so they could come back for more training. He thought if the student actually earned their pilots license, they'd have no reason to return, but as long as they don't have it, then they were potentially still a customer. Even with students who could cut it, we were continually encouraged to drag out the process, milking them of every cent they had. Todd had even been known to shut the door to his office during meetings with the instructors and inappropriately gesture as if he were milking a cow while peeking through the blinds to make sure none of the students could see him.

"Fill that bucket up, yeah," he'd say in the creepiest way possible.

Antonio fit his model perfectly. I'm pretty sure he had been turned down from several other flight schools, who most likely had told him that he needed to work on his English first before learning to fly. But, once again, Todd would take anyone who's paying.

"How is he going to communicate with ATC?" I asked. "Even people who speak English well have trouble getting used to the fast pace of ATC communications."

"Oh, I'm sure he'll be fine."

"Alright, whatever."

I cared, but it was hard to at times. When it came down to it, I guess my own flight time was all that really mattered to me. If Antonio wanted to pretend he knew English so he could get his parents to pay for a few months of him hanging out in Florida, and all Todd wanted was Antonio's parents' money, I suppose I was fine with getting the flight time I needed out of the situation. It was going to be a win for everyone.

I returned to the lobby to tell Antonio that we would begin flight training the following day. He didn't understand me, of course. I ended up having to take a calendar off the wall, and circle tomorrow's date on it while shouting, "Thursday!" Then I grabbed the clock off the wall and gave it to him. "Ten!" I said while pointing to the 10 on the clock. He nodded, I think in understanding, maybe. As he walked out of the building, taking the calendar and clock with him, I shouted, "See you tomorrow!"

He looked back at me in confusion, then smiled and held up his new clock and calendar. "Thank you. Ciao."

He probably thinks they're some sort of welcome gift. Oh well, guess I'd have to wait till tomorrow to see if he showed up.

-3-
The 92' Camry

I woke up in the morning to the sound of fourteen alarm clocks going off. There were twelve of us instructors living in a one-bedroom apartment because none of us could afford a place of our own. Flight instructor's pay is well below the national poverty level.

So, this is how we lived, like sardines, well beyond the max occupancy of this little apartment. "It's a crash pad," that's what we told people. That's what a bunch of broke pilots call it when they all pile into a tiny apartment because they can't afford anything else. I guess it made us feel a little better about living in squalor.

There were fourteen alarm clocks for the twelve of us because each of us had our own alarm clock, and one guy had three. He was afraid of oversleeping, so even though the room was filled with alarm clocks, he still set three of his own right next to his head just in case the other eleven in the room didn't work. Every night before bed he went through a ritual of setting and repeatedly checking each one. Then he'd lie down to sleep only to jump back up a few moments later in a panic to go through checking them all again. He would do this over and over, some nights for hours on end till he finally fell asleep. It was like the thought of oversleeping worried him so much that he couldn't sleep, making it far more likely that he would oversleep. It was ridiculous.

Every morning the noise from all of our alarm clocks was so loud I expected the neighbors to call the cops. I mean, it was so loud that if the fire alarm went off in the building, no one would be able to hear it.

I got out of my sleeping bag, and hopped over the other sleeping bags that lay in rows across the bedroom floor on my way to the bathroom. I had the first slot on the shower schedule this month. It was 6 a.m. I had five minutes of bathroom time. At 6:05 it would be the next person's turn to use our single bathroom. That meant peeing, taking a shit, showering, shaving, brushing your teeth, and whatever else you had to do in five minutes or less, every morning. Then I had to sit and wait until everyone else finished their turn. At 7 when all of us were ready, we would all pile into one car, like some sort of circus act, and drive to the airport. Dave was the only one of us who had a car. The rest of us couldn't afford one.

I was buried in student loans from flight school, and my salary as an instructor was barely paying the interest on them, along with my one-twelfth share of rent on the apartment. Between the twelve of us instructors our total student loan debt was well into the millions, and our phones were ringing constantly with calls from creditors.

That morning, after I finished showering, I got dressed in the living room. There was no privacy in this apartment and not much elbow room to get dressed either. We had to wear a white shirt, blue-and-green-striped tie, blue pants, and black shoes. I had one of each, which got washed on Sunday afternoons. It was Thursday, and my clothes were starting to stink, so I sprayed some Windex on them to freshen them up.

It was summer in Florida, and the planes we flew had no air conditioning. I came home every day soaking in sweat. We'd been petitioning Todd for months to let us wear polo shirts and shorts, maybe even tennis shoes, something more appropriate to our working conditions, but Todd wouldn't budge on his uniform policy. He claimed that he needed us looking professional. I didn't really see how a bunch of instructors wearing heavy polyester in South Florida and drenched in sweat was a professional look, but OK.

Once I was dressed, I sat down in one of the lawn chairs in our living room and ate my breakfast of Ramen Noodles while I waited for everyone else to get ready. We all ate Ramen Noodles for breakfast and dinner; it was all we could afford. For lunch we snuck into the FBO (Fixed Base Operator) next door to the flight school to steal popcorn and cookies. They knew what we were up to but I guess felt sorry enough for us that they never called us out on it.

When everyone was ready, we all piled into Dave's car. It was like putting a jigsaw puzzle together, but we did this every morning, so it went smoothly. Everyone knew their spot. It was something we had practiced on our days off to be sure we wouldn't be late on a work day. If an instructor quit and a new instructor was hired and joined the group, we sometimes had to reconfigure depending on their stature compared to the instructor they replaced. We often tried to persuade Todd to hire new instructors who were the same height and weight as their predecessor so a complete reconfiguration wouldn't be necessary.

Even though Dave was the only one of us lucky enough to own a car it was no gem. It was a '92 Camry he got from a salvage yard for a couple hundred bucks. It had been in a wreck where the airbags had deployed, so there were holes in the steering wheel and dash on the passenger side with just the edges of the airbags remaining where they had been cut out. The little bit of blood splatter still left on the dash was always a nice reminder to drive safe. On the outside the car was at least six different colors; it was impossible to determine what the original color had been. It looked like it had been pieced together from about five different cars. The windows were made of garbage bags and shipping tape and, naturally, the bumpers were held on with bungee cords.

Anytime another motorist caught a glimpse of us piled into our clown car, they did a double-take then stared in shock. Whenever Dave caught someone staring at us, he would un-tape the garbage bag that covered the driver's side window, wave at the people, and sing circus music just to add to their entertainment.

Dave's car had Missouri plates. He said the car was actually registered in New York, but he had a Colorado driver's license, and we were in Florida. Every one of us in the car probably had an ID from a different state. Pilot's live like gypsies so it's difficult to keep all your documentation pointing to one place. If we got pulled over like this, the cops would have a field day with us.

As wild as our situation was, though, we were far from being the most dangerous thing on the road in Southern Florida. With all the elderly snowbirds down here, it was an everyday occurrence to see cars slow rolling through red lights that appeared to be ghost riding with no driver. Just a tuft of white hair visible through the window as they passed by at 5 mph, completely unaware they were running a red light, maybe not even aware the car was moving at all.

This particular morning, on the road leading to the airport, the Lincoln Town Car in front of us was stopping at every single street sign. The passenger, an elderly woman, would get out of the car to read each sign closer. "*Speed Limit 35*," the sign read. Then she would get back in the car and they continued on at no more than 10 mph until reaching the next sign a mile or so down the road, abruptly stopping again, as if they almost hadn't seen it till the last second. The woman would get out of the car to read the sign. "Speed Limit 35, it says," we could hear her shout to her husband as she climbed back into the car.

This went on for miles. They continued to stop and read each sign along the road before continuing. Obviously, they were a bit near sighted and not able to read them from in the car as they passed.

"It's a good thing we left early today," I announced. We were stuck behind them; a median filled with palm trees and landscaping ran down the middle of the road, giving us no way to get around. Eventually, we reached a four-way intersection and the Town Car made a left turn through the intersection without stopping. *They must not have seen the bright red stop sign.*

Arriving at the airport, we disassembled our jigsaw puzzle in the reverse order from that which we assembled it, then filed into the flight school to start our day.

-4-
The King James Checklist

George was already outside preflighting the airplane. I hung out in the flight instructor's office for a few minutes drinking coffee.

Ian came in a few minutes later; he was the only instructor who didn't live in our little sardine-can fraternity. He had a place of his own, and the rest of us couldn't understand how he afforded it.

Ian was Todd's personal sidekick. He was in the US on a work visa that was dependent on this job. He had been unable to obtain a medical certificate in his home country of England due to some medical condition. None of us knew what his condition was, but rumor had it that Todd had paid off a doctor in the US to approve Ian's medical, and in return Ian had to do anything Todd asked. The rest of us all knew there was something shady going on with him; we just weren't exactly sure what. He was also the only instructor with his own office. The rest of us had to share an office. But he still stopped by our cramped little space regularly to try and hang out with us. He wanted to be part of our group, but none of us wanted him around.

He would try and make small talk with us and be friends but at the same time acted like he was above us, often speaking to us as if he were God's Gift to Aviation, a know-it-all. He got this attitude because he had been working there forever. I guess maybe he had seen it all, but we just looked down on him with pity.

In fact, behind his back we called him "The Lifer" because for all the rest of us, this was just a temporary job; for him, though, it was for life. He had more than enough flight time to not be an instructor anymore, but for some reason he couldn't leave. And so he became Todd's "yes man."

As Ian stood there and bragged about how much multi-time he had, the same as he did every morning, I looked out the window and saw that George was sitting in the plane. He looked like he was ready to go, so I grabbed my headset and headed outside. But as I approached the plane I could see that it was still tied down to the ramp. I opened the door to the plane, popped my head in, and saw that George was already buckled in. "You all done preflighting?" I asked.

"Yup, I'm ready," he said.

"You sure?" I asked. "Everything on the outside is ready to go? You did the full walk around?"

"Yup," he responded. "Everything's ready."

"OK," I said and climbed in. "Go ahead and start the checklist." I figured I'd turn this into a learning experience. And so, George began the checklist…

The checklists used in the real world by airline pilots are short and to the point, usually just one page that covers every phase of flight. They are made up of one- or two-word call-and-response items; common sense items and details are left out. But student pilots have to use a ridiculously long "King James Version" of the checklist, which goes into elaborate detail on every single item. I still find it funny that a highly complex jumbo-jet uses a one-page checklist, while a single-engine trainer that only has, like, four switches uses a twenty-page checklist that could almost be classified as literature. Here's an example:

Engine Start Checklist – King James Version

And the Lord spoke, saying, "In the beginning was thy throttle lever, and thy throttle lever was cracked to one-half inch. The crack of thy throttle lever was, in fact, one-half inch, no more, no less.

Thou shalt now turn thy electric fuel pump to the on position, mayest not be off, but on. For thy electric fuel pump is now in the on position; thou shalt now confirm thy electric fuel pump to be in the on position. Proceed further only if thy electric fuel pump shall not be off, but on.

Mixture is thy lever to be found in the lean position and advanced to the rich position. Once moved to the rich position, and in the rich position, thou shalt proceed. Fear not, ye, if thy mixture is found to be in the lean position still, thou shalt not proceed further, but move thy mixture lever to the rich position, then mayest thou proceed.

Thou shalt now move thy magneto switch to start. Passed left, passed right, passed both, to start. Thy magneto switch shall not remain in the off position, nor the left, nor the right, nor the both. In the start position, and held there till thy engine births a fire; then, and only then, thou shalt release thy magneto switch. Where, spring-loaded to both, it shall remain for the life of thy engines fire.

Go forth in thy quest to thy after-start procedures checklist, but do so only once thy oil lines be merry with pressure."

This went on for pages, and the student had to complete the whole checklist before we could fly. Most got the hang of it after a while, but George was as slow now as he was on his first day. On a good day, it took him upwards of twenty minutes to complete the whole checklist. Most days, by the time he got through the whole thing, we barely had any time to fly anymore.

When he was finally finished, he released the brakes to taxi, but of course we didn't move. He ran the power up a bit to get the plane going, still nothing. "Everything alright?" I asked.

"Yup," he said, as he firewalled it. The plane was fighting the ropes with every single horse power it had. He even started scooting back and forth in his seat in some sort of effort to rock the plane out of our parking spot.

As funny as this was, I had to stop him. Much more of this would probably rip the tie downs right out of the concrete. "Hang on," I said as I grabbed his hand, pulling the throttle to idle.

"I think the brakes are jammed," he said.

"The brakes aren't jammed," I told him.

"Well, we're not moving."

"It's not the brakes. What else could be holding us down?"

"I don't know. The parking brake?"

"It's not the brakes."

"Well then, I don't know." He was getting frustrated.

"Why don't you shut it down and get out and preflight again," I suggested.

"OK," he said as he grabbed the checklist and announced, "Engine shut down checklist."

I grabbed it from him, pulled the mixture, and with one swipe down the panel shut everything off. "There you go. Engine shut down checklist complete," I announced. "Go preflight again."

George unbuckled, got out, and walked around the plane. His eyes kept drifting toward the brakes. "It's not the brakes!" I yelled from the window.

He continued around the whole plane without noticing anything that alerted him. "I don't see anything," he said. "The brakes look fine."

He just wouldn't give up about the brakes; he was so focused on that being the problem that he still didn't see the ropes tying the plane the ground. "Do you see any ropes?" I asked.

"Oh yeah, I forgot those" he said.

George untied the ropes and climbed back in the plane. "Can I start the checklist again?" he asked.

"You sure we're ready this time?"

"Yup, I think so."

"Go ahead then."

George began the ridiculously long checklist again. "Place thy seat belt into thy buckle," he started.

"Wait, gimme the checklist." I said as I grabbed it out of his hand. "Put your seat belt on, and start this thing."

"But I need the checklist," he whined.

"You don't need the checklist; you've flown this plane enough that you should be able to start it without the checklist."

"What do I do first?"

"Crack the throttle, turn the fuel pump on, put the mixture rich, and crank it," I told him.

"OK," he said, sounding very nervous. "The throttle's cracked, the fuel pump's on, the mixture is lean. Now what?"

"Put it to rich."

"What?"

"The mixture, put it to rich."

He moved the mixture lever forward. "OK, the mixture is rich. Now what?"

"Just crank it."

"Passed left, passed right, passed both," George mumbled as he cranked the starter, and the engine fired up. He seemed amazed with himself, like it was some sort of major accomplishment to start an engine without his trusty checklist. "What's next?"

"What do you normally do after starting the engine?"

"I don't know. What?"

"Check the engine gauges. Make sure you've got oil pressure."

"Oh yeah, right. Make sure thy oil lines be merry with pressure," he said as he leaned down, inspecting each gauge one at a time. But as he did this, his feet slipped off the pedals, and he released the brakes. The plane started rolling forward across the ramp, and George was completely unaware. We rolled fifty feet before George picked his head up and looked around. "We're moving," he said in amazement.

"I know. Why are we moving?"

"The brakes aren't on," he responded as we continued to roll.

I let him know he could, "Go ahead and stop us whenever you feel like it."

"Oh OK," and George hit the brakes, bringing us to an abrupt stop.

I had to explain to him what had happened, "You released the brakes when you put your head down."

"Well, normally when I put my head down the parking brake is on," he defended.

"Well, then why didn't you put the parking brake on?"

"'Cause I don't have the checklist that tells me to. Thou shalt now engage thy parking brake."

"Here," I said, and I gave George the checklist back. He obviously didn't have enough common sense to not use it. He continued with his checklist for another twenty minutes. It got to the point where he still wasn't ready to taxi, and we were running out of time. "By the time we take-off, we're just going to have to head right back," I told him. "I think we need to just go park it and call it a day."

-5-
Airworthiness and Registration Please

It was 10 a.m. on Thursday, still no sign of Antonio. I waited around in the lobby for fifteen minutes or so to see if he showed. Not to my surprise, he didn't. Most of the other instructors were already outside getting ready to depart with their 10 a.m. students, and the building was starting to get quiet. Since Antonio hadn't shown, I wouldn't be flying this slot, which meant I wouldn't be paid.

Instructors only get paid for flight time, which meant from the time the brakes were released and the plane started moving with the intention of flight till the plane was parked, we got paid. Any time spent on the ground in between flights was off the clock. If we had an open flight slot during the day, we made nothing but still were not allowed to leave the flight school. I don't know of any other job where an employer could get away with having rules like this. No one else in any other profession would put up with it. Most days I worked for ten hours but was usually only paid for five or six. Even on the best days, pay maxed out at eight hours because that's the legal daily limit on flight time. And to actually get eight hours of flight time, and eight hours of pay, usually meant working a twelve- to fourteen-hour day.

The fact that Antonio hadn't shown was cutting into my paycheck, and I wasn't happy about it. I knew this was going to be a problem. The one safeguard instructors have for their pay if a student doesn't show is charging them a no-call no-show, and that's exactly what I was going to do. I could charge Antonio for thirty minutes of flight time as a penalty, and I would get thirty minutes of pay. This would still be a loss because had we actually flown, we would have flown for more than thirty minutes, but at least it was something. It still meant nothing in my logbook, though, and that was really the only reason I was here.

For Todd, though, no-call no-shows were his bread and butter. He got to charge the student without having to put any wear and tear on the aircraft or use any fuel. He was going to see this as great news.

"Todd, Antonio hasn't shown." I said as I poked my head into his office. He was busy shredding documents as usual. "Do you have a contact number for him?"

"He didn't show, huh? Guess we'll charge him a no-call no-show," Todd said with a grin.

"Yea, that's what I was going to do," I said, "but I'd still like to try and get him here. Do you have a number?"

"Hang on a second," Todd said while focused on his computer screen. "Here's the number to his hotel room. Ready?"

"Go," I said.

Todd read the phone number to me, and I punched it in my phone. I stepped out into the hallway to make the call.

The phone rang a few times. "*Salve,*" Antonio answered.

"Antonio, this is your flight instructor," I said. "You're supposed to be at the airport to fly."

"No Inglese." He said, which was not a surprise. *Could I use this as a confession?*

"Antonio, airport!" I yelled.

"No Inglese, arrivederci." And he hung up.

Well, that's great.

I walked back into Todd's office. "Did you get a hold of him?" Todd asked.

"Yup," I said, "but all he kept saying was 'no English,' so I doubt he's showing up."

"Well, he'll come back in eventually."

"Yeah, we'll see."

"Hey, in the meantime just keep putting him on your schedule and keep charging him no-call no-shows." Todd acted as if we were on some great path to riches with this advice. But for me this was the second time today that I wasn't going to be getting any flight time.

Later that night, I woke up to the sound of my phone ringing. Glancing at the clock, I saw that it was 10 p.m.. I jumped up out of my sleeping bag and hopped over five other bags on my way to the hallway. "Hello," I answered.

"Hey, it's Todd. I need you come down to the airport. Antonio's here to fly."

"What?"

"Antonio just showed up. Apparently he thought you meant 10 p.m., I need you to come down here and fly with him."

"But I'm sleeping, and I don't have any way to get there. Dave's asleep, and he has the car."

"Well, get up and find a way. Hurry, he's waiting."

"Fine, what are you doing at the airport this late anyway?"

"Ah, I just stayed late to finish up some paperwork."

"OK, I'm on my way." I paused for a second, thinking about waking Dave up to borrow the Camry. He was sound asleep in the sleeping bag next to mine, and he didn't like being woken up. *Better not.* "I'm going to have to walk though, so it's going to be a while," I told Todd.

I ran all the way to the airport. By the time I got there I was completely out of breath. Todd was sitting at the front desk in the lobby when I walked in. "Hurry up, he's sitting in the plane waiting for you." He seemed irritated that it took me so long to get to airport. "I already had the plane fueled up; it's ready to go. Get going." He motioned toward the door.

I walked out to the ramp to find Antonio sitting in the plane, in the dark, by himself. He had never flown before, and usually on the first day of flight training we teach students how to preflight before anything else. It was dark out, though; it was late, and I was in no mood for this. I decided I would just preflight the plane myself and take him up for a ride for a while. There was no way I could teach him anything of value on his very first flight in the dark anyway. But as long as I was here, I may as well get some flight time and some pay out of it.

I did a quick walk around, checked the fuel and oil, and jumped in the plane with him. I reached into the seat pocket to grab the binder with the plane's log books, and when I did, I noticed that the clear plastic pocket where the airworthiness and registration certificates for the plane are kept was empty. *Maybe they fell out.*

I started searching under the seats for them, but they were nowhere to be found. I tried to get Antonio to help me look, but he had no idea what I was doing. He just sat there looking confused when I said, "Missing papers."

After tearing the plane apart for several minutes looking, I gave up. They weren't here, and we couldn't fly this plane without them. "I'll be right back," I told Antonio.

Todd was still sitting at the front desk when I came back inside. "The airworthiness and registration certificates for thirty foxtrot alpha are missing," I informed him.

"Oh, maybe someone took them home as a souvenir." Todd didn't seem surprised or concerned at all by this. "Go ahead and take the plane anyway; it's fine."

"I can't go without them," I told him, shocked that he would even suggest it. "They have to be there."

"Oh, don't worry. It's fine. You have my permission. You're all set, go ahead"

I didn't know how to respond. For a second, I looked at him with a question. "No, it doesn't matter if I have your permission; they're required by law. The plane can't be flown without them."

"No problem, I'll have a new set faxed over in the morning."

"OK, well then can we get a different plane to fly tonight?" I asked.

"No, I already had that one fueled up," he responded. "You can take that one."

I was starting to get pissed. "I'm not taking that one," I said firmly. "Let me take another plane, or I'm not going."

We continued to argue back and forth for several minutes. All the while Antonio still sat in the plane outside, waiting. Todd wouldn't budge, though. He was getting angrier by the minute, and I was starting to worry he might fire me. Just then Antonio walked into the lobby. He said something to us in Italian that neither of us understood, but I think he was trying to tell us he was tired of waiting and was going home. Todd grabbed a piece of paper off the counter and slid it toward Antonio, "Sign this," he said and handed him a pen.

Antonio looked at the piece of paper as Todd pointed at the signature line on the bottom and drew an X next to it. "Sign here," Todd repeated.

Antonio signed it and set the pen down on the counter.

"What was it?" I asked after Antonio left.

"Oh, I just got him to pay for two hours of flight time," Todd said, obviously proud of himself. "He didn't know what he was signing."

"I thought you said he could read English?" I questioned, already knowing the answer.

"Go home! And be glad I don't fire you."

All I could think about on my long walk home was how little concern Todd had that such important documentation was missing. And I thought, he probably knew why they were missing.

The next time I was assigned to fly that plane, a few days later, I saw that the certificates were back in the pocket where they belonged. But when I pulled them out to examine them it was obvious that they were a photocopy of certificates from another plane and the tail number for the plane they came from had been whited out and typed over with the tail number for this plane.

I knew it wasn't legit, but what was I going to do? If I got ramp checked by the FAA, I'd just have to play dumb. I was quickly learning that being able to play dumb was going to be a necessary part of this job.

-6-
Simulated Engine Failure

The stall horn was going off again. We were fifty feet off the ground and fifty degrees nose up. Apparently, George thought this would be the best time to practice his stall recoveries. He didn't really think that; this was just his way of taking off, and we were not in an F-14, so this wasn't going to work. Every takeoff he would rotate and rip back on the yoke until it reached the stop and then hold it there with a death grip.

"Pitch down a little," I told him for the millionth time, while pushing forward on the yoke to overpower him and lower the nose. "Right there, about seven degrees. Just hold it there." But as soon as I let go, he was pulling back again.

"But I feel the need…The need for speed," he'd say.

"Not in this plane, you don't," I'd tell him. We would do this back and forth, over and over, on every takeoff. He would pull back till the stall horn sounded, and then I would push forward to get the pitch back to where it should be. As soon as I let go, he would pull back again. Sometimes I would throw caution to the wind and let him stall it. Even then he wouldn't let the nose down, he would continue holding the yoke at full lock, aggravating the stall, until I yelled, "MY AIRPLANE!" took the controls, and recovered just before we turned into a smoking hole in the tarmac. But even a near death experience didn't seem to scare him away from his *Top Gun*-style takeoffs.

We would eventually make it up to a safe altitude, and once we got there, if I asked him to demonstrate a stall recovery for me. Asking him to pull back and to pitch the plane up on purpose until we stalled and then demonstrate the proper recovery, something every student needed to know how to do. He wouldn't do it. He was too afraid to stall the plane. He would pull back a little, and then immediately shove the nose back forward violently and say, "There, I did it."

"That wasn't a stall," I'd tell him. "You've got to pitch up more than that and hold it longer."

He seemed to have no problem with this maneuver at dangerously low altitudes where we should definitely not be doing it. But at a safe altitude where there was plenty of time to recover, no way, he refused. It was mind boggling.

"Alright then, let's move on to something else," I suggested. "How about some turns around a point?" This is another rudimentary maneuver used to teach proper handling of an airplane, something he really needed to work on.

"No," he whined, "I don't want to do this stuff. I just want to practice landings so I can go solo."

I wanted to tell him, "You're probably not ever going solo," but I couldn't crush his spirit. Plus, Todd would never approve of my discouraging a student from continuing on. George's family seemed to have an endless amount of money to throw away on his flight training, and he could potentially be a lifelong customer for Todd.

"How about we go down to Coral Island and do some pattern work so you can practice your landings," I suggested. "If you want to solo then that's what we need to work on."

George agreed.

I told him to switch over to the advisory frequency for Coral Island and begin making position reports as we approached the airport.

Since they didn't have a control tower at Coral Island because it wasn't busy enough to warrant one, aircraft operating near the airport self-control themselves by communicating directly with other aircraft in the area over an advisory frequency.

George fumbled with his chart for a while trying to find the frequency that he should have memorized by now, since we went to this airport literally every single day. Eventually, I just had to punch it into the radio for him since we were getting close, and he still hadn't been able to locate it on his chart.

His next step was to listen to the automated weather report for the airport, find out what the winds were doing, and decide which runway we should land on. I ended up having to give him the frequency for this as well since he still hadn't been able to locate Coral Island on his chart.

The automated weather played on repeat, over and over on our com two as George stared into the distance, seemingly trying to take in the information and decide which runway we should use and how we should enter the traffic pattern. During this time, he seemed to be completely oblivious to how close to the airport we were getting. I was already making position reports over the advisory frequency to alert any other aircraft in the area that we were approaching because he was neglecting to do it, and by the time he got his shit together and decided to do it, we would already be there.

This was popular among students. If they got overwhelmed, they would just completely ignore communicating with other aircraft or air traffic control. And when I would jump in and do it, they seemed to not even notice, or maybe they were content with me taking some work load off their plate. It sure wasn't helping his chances of going solo, though. If you're not going to talk to ATC when I'm here watching, you're probably not going to talk to them when I'm not here either.

After the eighth time the automated weather repeated, I shut it off. *I think he should have heard it by now.* "Which runway are you using?" I asked.

"Ah, I missed the wind. Can you put that back on again?"

"How did you miss it? It repeated like ten times. The wind's one nine zero at eleven," I informed him.

"Ah?"

"You've got runway three-five or one-seven."

"Ah?"

"If the wind's at one nine zero, which runway would point closest to the direction of the wind?"

"Ah, one-seven?" He sounded unsure, and I know he was guessing, but he was correct.

We went through the usual routine of his not seeing the airport and not being able to decide how to enter the traffic pattern. At one point he saw it but still hadn't made up his mind on what he was going to do next. All the while, I was still giving our position reports over advisory since he wasn't going to bother to. There didn't seem to be anyone else in the area; at least, no one else was responding, so I just let George do his thing for as long as it took. At least we weren't in anyone else's way out here.

This airport usually wasn't very busy. Typically, it was just a few student pilots and instructors using it to practice landings, and occasionally a private jet would fly in. It was surrounded by swamp, and alligators often came out onto the runway in the afternoon to lie on the warm asphalt and sun themselves. You had to keep an eye out for them because their dark color blended in with the runway, and sometimes they were hard to see until you got pretty close. If there was one out there, the airport authority had a guy that would drive out on the runway in a van and chase it off.

By the time George decided how he was going to enter the traffic pattern we had flown over and past the airport. We were now ten miles southeast, and he had lost sight of it again.

Eventually, after a lot of circling and a lot of help from me, we managed to make it into the traffic pattern. On downwind and abeam the numbers, George pulled the throttle back, extended a notch of flaps, and completed the King James Before-Landing

Checklist during which he switched the electric fuel pump and landing light on. Moments later, he panicked.

"Ah, before landing checklist. Sorry, I forgot," he said apparently forgetting he had already completed the checklist like thirty seconds ago. He went through it again. Except this time, he turned both the electric fuel pump and landing light back off. He obviously wasn't paying any attention to the position of the switches, he was just blindly flipping them. I flipped them both back on when he wasn't looking. I'd mention it to him later during our post-flight briefing, but now wasn't the time. If I broke what little concentration he had, he'd lose sight of the airport again, and we'd be back to another twenty minutes of circling and trying to figure out where we were.

George banked the plane left, turning base to final, and extended another notch of flaps. Just then I noticed another airplane on the south side of the airport that appeared to be on final approach for runway three-five, the same runway we were landing on but coming from the opposite direction.

"Anyone else in the pattern at Coral?" I asked over the radio but got no response. George hadn't noticed. He was probably too busy thinking about how he wasn't going to flare during landing and wheelbarrow this thing onto the runway.

"Go around," I announced.

Nothing.

"My airplane, we're going around," I said as I grabbed the controls and firewalled the throttle. I keyed up the mic. "Coral traffic, four foxtrot alphas' going around," I announced as I veered us right of the runway while climbing. The plane approaching from the other direction appeared to be continuing to land. It didn't seem like they even saw us.

"Did I do something wrong?" George asked.

"Look out to your left," I told him. "See the traffic."

The other aircraft was touching down on the runway as we passed by them in a climb, and I could read the tail number on the side of the plane. It was one of ours. I made a few more attempts to communicate with them over the radio, both on the advisory frequency and also on our company's frequency, which they should have been monitoring on their second radio as well, with no response. Whoever it was, they were landing with an eleven-knot tailwind, which is not something a student pilot should be doing, and not speaking to anyone. It had to be a student flying solo.

I radioed Todd over our company frequency. "Who's flying six foxtrot alpha?"

"Ah, that's Ian's student going solo." He responded. *Figures.*

"Well, he's down here in Coral going the wrong way in the pattern, doing touch-and-goes with a tailwind, and not speaking to anyone, FYI."

"OK, sounds good." Todd answered back. He obviously didn't care.

This is why we never sent two students solo at the same time. They would for sure get into a midair or collide on the runway because neither of them would be speaking to each other or looking out for other aircraft around them. And if I had known that Ian had sent someone solo, I would have steered clear of wherever they were going because he would just send anyone, ready or not.

"Let's go up to Calusa and do pattern work up there," I told George. We still had some time to kill, but I wasn't staying here, not around this guy who was obviously oblivious to his surroundings.

"OK," George agreed.

As usual, he spent the next thirty minutes trying to figure out how to get us to Calusa. We were just flying in circles again out over the eastern side of Marbella. Now it was getting to the point that if we ever made it there, there wasn't going to be any time to do anything except turn around and come back anyway, and I was getting bored.

I pulled the throttle to idle. "Engine failure," I announced. This would be a little more entertaining.

This was a routine training exercise for students. When you're flying a plane that only has only one engine, you need to always be aware of your surroundings and thinking about where you would try to land if the engine quit. Obviously, an airport is always the best choice, but if there's no airport within gliding distance, an open field or even a road might be your only option. Students have to demonstrate that they can quickly make a decision on where to put the plane down and maneuver as necessary to get it there in one shot because if you miss judge it, there's no trying again.

George always wanted a redo. I would tell him, "Nope, you died that time, but you'll get another shot to show you can do it when you least expect it." Now was that time.

"Set your pitch for best glide and let me know where you're going," I told him.

We were diving. We had already lost fifteen hundred feet because he was pitching the nose forward while trying to look for a place to land out in front of us, completely neglecting to maintain the proper airspeed which would slow our rate of descent and give him more gliding distance. I helped him with the trim because if I didn't, this was just going to be a complete waste of time. "How about that field right there?" I pointed to a large, open grassy field.

He didn't respond, but he did turn toward the field. He was pouring sweat. "I'm going to make it this time. You just watch," he told me.

"I'm watching. You just watch your airspeed; we're going down fast."

He wasn't maintaining the best glide speed, though, and was losing altitude quicker than he should. As we got lower, it became apparent he wasn't going to make the field that I had pointed out.

"How about that one? I can make that one," he said in a panic, pointing to a much smaller field, next to a supermarket parking lot. It was much closer to us but near a busy area, and it was a small field, less than ideal. A few minutes ago, he had several other choices that would have been better than this, but now as low as he was, this was probably his only option left.

"OK, if you think that's going to work."

He maneuvered toward the field, but he wasn't going to make it there either. On the path he was on he was going to put it down short of the field on a busy road. We were getting low. At a certain point, when you know it's not going to work out for them, you have to call the exercise off and climb out.

"Full throttle. Go around," I told him.

But I got no response. "George, go around!"

Suddenly, he snapped out of his trance and slammed the throttle forward like he was freakin' He-Man, and when he did, all I heard was a *snap*.

It broke. The throttle cable broke.

"MY AIRPLANE!" I grabbed the controls. The engine was still running, but there was no power. I moved the throttle lever back and forth, nothing. It was stuck at idle. We were going down for real.

I held the glide the best I could. It looked like I was going to clear the road, but there was no way I was clearing the fence that lay between us and the field on the other side. Going through it was the only option.

I pulled the mixture just as we passed over the road, killing the engine and hoping to avoid a fire. Cars were swerving and slamming on their brakes below us.

George yelled, "I'm punching out! Eject! Eject! Eject!"

"There's no ejection seats, you dumbass! Brace for impact!"

We crashed through the chain-link fence, which tangled in the prop and immediately came ripping through the windscreen, the metal wire thrashing through the cockpit.

The landing gear impacted hard in the rough, overgrown field. I held the yoke back at full lock and stood on the brakes as we bounced to a stop with the nose gear buckled and the prop buried in the dirt.

For a few moments, it was silence.

"You alright?" I asked George. His face was bleeding, and he had some cuts, but he otherwise looked OK.

"I'm fine, I think," he responded.

I had cuts on my hands and face too, from the fence coming through the windscreen, but it was minor. We were both OK and were able to walk away from it. *It was a good landing.*

The plane was totaled, though. The prop was trashed; the nose gear had mangled the firewall, and both wings were smashed to hell from impacting fence posts.

I could hear sirens in the distance, and people from the road were running toward us to help. *Shit, the certificates,* was the first thing that came to mind. *Are they even valid?* I pondered for a moment about quickly setting the plane on fire, but when I reached into the side pocket and pulled them out, they looked real. "I think this plane's legit," I told George. "It's my lucky day, looks like I won't have to burn the evidence."

You would think Todd would have been upset about his plane being totaled, but he wasn't. Not even a little bit. In fact, his mood was more so celebratory. The plane was a piece of junk, and he had a lot of insurance on it. Within a couple days he had another P.O.S. 1960s Warrior sitting on the ramp to replace it. "Bought it in South America," he told me with a wink. "Cost me less than what the insurance company is paying out. I think I might buy myself a new car."

And he did. A few days later Todd was driving a new BMW M5.

-7-

The Instructor of the Month vs. The Prince of El Salvador

Todd named me instructor of the month following the accident—not because George and I survived the crash, of course. It was because it got him the nice new BMW. Ian had been named instructor of the month for every month I'd worked there, and from what I'd heard he had been instructor of the month every month since the flight school opened, so this was the first time any of the rest of us had received the honor.

It came with perks. I actually got to take a break from flying with George, and Todd even passed Antonio off to another instructor. He still hadn't shown up for a flight lesson. But regardless, Todd had been putting him on my schedule twice a day for a couple months and charging him for no-call no-shows. At least now he was going to start putting him on someone else's schedule, so maybe I could get a student that would actually show up and fly. That way I could get flight time and be paid instead of having to sit around for two flight slots a day doing nothing and making nothing.

Instead, Todd gave me a couple instrument students, which was a nice change of pace. At least these students had made it as far as getting their private pilot's license, so they were proven to be at least somewhat capable. Instrument training was a whole other thing, though, and it had a way of making students who seemed decent before turn into idiots.

There was a big weeding-out process as the students progressed. Many who made it to the point of getting their private license never made it past that and gave up before ever earning their instrument rating. Commercial training weeded out more, and by the time a student made it to multi training, he was like one of a hundred. In fact, we only had one multi-engine airplane at the school, that's how few multi students there were.

It was a Seminole, and it was Ian's personal plane because he hogged all the multi students. I would have to wreck a lot more planes and rack up several more months of instructor of the month before I got anywhere near it. And I'm not sure I could or wanted to compete with Ian on that anyway, although I have to admit I was thinking about putting a few more Warriors through fences if that's what it took to get some multi time.

Ian would get his throne back soon enough, though. His specialty was losing students in either the ocean or the everglades. He would sign students off for solo cross-counties. Then they were never to be seen or heard from again.

Just the month prior he had signed a private student off for a solo flight from Marbella to Key West. The student never made it to Key West. I don't know who in their right mind would ever think it would be a good idea to send someone with so little experience, in a single engine plane, out over the ocean where they would have no visible landmarks and nothing but a VFR sectional to navigate with. But the student wanted to visit Key West, and Ian thought it was a good idea.

Apparently so did Todd. In fact, I think this was Todd's ideal situation: a plane and all its documentation lost at sea. Plus, there was no wreckage to be found for his insurance company to argue that the plane wasn't in mint condition before the wreck, thereby increasing his payout.

Either way I was going to enjoy not flying with George while it lasted. However, this instrument student I had today wasn't going to be any easier.

His name was Nelson. He came from El Salvador, and he thought he knew more than I did. This happens often once a student earns their private pilot's license; they think they know everything and don't need instruction anymore. I had more than ten times the flight time this kid had, and I didn't know everything, so I doubted he did either.

To make matters worse, his dad was the owner of the national airline of El Salvador, and Nelson reportedly had a captain's position waiting for him when he got back home with his certificates. No building time, no time as an FO, straight to captain of any plane he wanted. Must be nice.

His previous instructor had already warned me this kid had a chip on his shoulder, so at least I knew what I was getting into with him. It didn't make it any less aggravating, though.

"Did you read the assigned chapter in your book last night?" I asked during our preflight briefing. I already knew the answer.

Some students thought they could fake their way through not preparing for the lesson, but it was obvious when they didn't read the assigned materials. It also meant we would have to waste time on the ground so I could explain to him what he should have read on his own time. If I didn't, he wasn't going to understand what we were doing once we got up in the air, and it would be pointless because I'd have to spend the whole time up there telling him things he could have learned in a book.

While I explained to him the lesson for the day. "Yeah, yeah, I know, I know," was all he kept repeating while he rolled his eyes at me and played on his phone, ignoring everything I had to say. Even though he did have thirty-five hours under the hood, he had never flown in actual instrument conditions before, yet apparently, he knew it all and had seen it all.

The hood is a visor that students wear to block their view outside the plane to simulate instrument conditions during training. Up to this point that was the only instrument time Nelson had under his belt, simulated. And while the hood worked as a training device, it wasn't perfect. Students could cheat and peek around the sides if they want to, but if they did that, they were really only cheating themselves out of learning to fly instruments. That was all Nelson had been doing up to this point. The instructor who had flown with Nelson through the first thirty-five hours of his training told me that he had been peeking out the side of the visor the entire time.

Today was going to be different, though. The skies were overcast with 500-foot ceilings, and it was raining. It was going to be Nelson's first time in actual so there was no way he could cheat or fake it.

The hood wouldn't be necessary as this was the real deal. He had already suggested to me that he was ready for his checkride during the preflight briefing. *We'll see how ready he feels after this flight.*

When we finished the preflight briefing, he suggested that I go preflight the plane while he waited in the lobby out of the rain. "Yeah, that's not going to happen," I told him. "You're the student; you need to do the preflight."

"Look, I'm sitting in the left seat; your sitting in the right seat," he told me. "I've got my license now, so you're my bitch. I don't need you instructors telling me what to do anymore, and I don't need to be preflighting anymore either. I know how to do it so that's your job now. It's the PIC's responsibility to delegate tasks to his underlings."

"Listen, dude, you don't have your instrument rating. You're still in training. I'm your instructor; I'm the PIC; you're the student; you go preflight, or we don't fly."

"Fine, you bitch, whatever, I'll be waiting in the plane, and don't forget to carry my bag out for me. If you don't, I'll tell my dad, and he'll see to it that Todd fires you."

We hadn't even gotten in the plane yet, and I was ready to light this kid up. I really wanted to just cancel on him and tell him sorry but we're not flying until you change your attitude, but I thought I'd get the chance to put him in his place once we were in the air. He wanted to peek out the visor thinking he's going to skate through this without learning how to do it. He was about to learn there's no peeking in actual.

Once airborne and climbing, we entered the cloud layer, and he was immediately disoriented. Within seconds we were in a hard banking descent. I had to grab the controls and fight him to get us out of the unusual attitude we were in and back to a normal climb.

"You messed me up by grabbing the controls," he tried to argue, thinking he was going to blame me for his loss of control. "This is so stupid anyway. Why doesn't this plane have autopilot? It's so unsophisticated."

"Because this is how you learn the basics. You wouldn't learn anything flying around with an autopilot on."

"I'm not like you. I'm not going to have to fly a piece of shit like this around for the rest of my life. I'll be flying the best planes in the world."

"That's fine, but you still need to learn how to fly without automation first. Here, you ready to try again?"

"Yes. I didn't need you helping me in the first place."

"Fair enough. Your airplane." And I let go of the yoke.

But he was immediately losing control again. ATC gave us a vector, and in his attempt to make the turn, we wound up knife-edge in a thousand-foot-per-minute descent. There was no way he was doing this on his own. I ended up having to help him the entire flight. He was far worse off than I had thought. He couldn't even keep us straight and level. Approaches were completely out of the question. Basically after a few minutes I was flying, and he just had his hands on the controls acting like he was flying. He had reached the point pretty quickly that he knew he couldn't do it and was just letting me fly. He wasn't going to admit to it, though, and he even later tried to take credit for the approaches.

"Told you I could do it," he said during our post flight briefing. "Now will you sign me off for my checkride already?"

I tried to argue with him that he was nowhere near ready, especially since I had just flown the entire flight because he couldn't keep control of the plane for more than a few seconds. But he kept arguing back that he had done it all.

Some days, with students like this I felt like I should have let them crash us just so that when we're sitting there, mangled in the wreckage, I could use my last breath to say, "I told you so." You wouldn't believe how many times after I've saved us from certain doom, a student tried to not only argue that everything would have been fine and they never needed my help, but also actually suggest that it was somehow my fault or ATC's fault that they were losing control in the first place.

"You can blame whomever you want for your screw-ups now," I told him, "but when the day comes that I'm not here with you, do you really think you're going to make it on your own? The bottom line is you need more training. You need about three and a half more hours of instrument time minimum anyway before you can be signed off, and I don't think that that's going to be anywhere near enough. You don't even have a limited grasp on basic aircraft control, and you're a long ways off from successfully flying an ILS down to minimums. Going forward, I suggest you take it seriously and not cheat at it because you're not learning anything that way. And today obviously proved that. Every time I let go of the controls you were in an unusual attitude within seconds. Do you really think you would have survived up there without me?"

"Listen, you bitch. You think you're hot stuff because you know how to fly these little prop planes. Who cares? I'm never going to need to know how to do any of this stuff anyway cause my dad owns an airline, and when I leave here, he's already got me a job as captain on a triple-seven and that's a real airplane. It has autopilot that flies itself, it even lands itself. It's not one of your little training planes that you have to do everything by hand like this is the olden days. You're just jealous cause you know I'm going to be flying something you'll never get to, and you're going to be stuck flying these little planes for pennies while I'm up above you, kicked back in my captain's seat, getting served by my flight attendants, while my co-pilot does all the bitch work. I don't need to know this stuff because in the planes I'm going to be flying I won't need to. If you're lucky, you can be my co-pilot and do my bitch work, bitch."

He was probably right. It's not about how good a pilot you are; it's all about who you know. He came from a rich family in El Salvador, one that owned an entire airline. When he went back home with his certificates, he would be put right into a position flying an advanced jumbo jet without ever having to go through what I'm doing to earn my way there. It would just be handed to him. All he needed from us was some pieces of paper that said he knew how to fly. He didn't really need to learn anything, and he probably never would have to demonstrate his ability to fly instruments on a rudimentary level like this ever again. Any check airman that ever tests him along the way would be paid to look the other way and push the papers through.

When Todd found out I was giving Nelson a hard time, he was pissed. "Don't you know who his family is? Your job is to get him the hours he needs to take his checkride. Sign him off, and I'll make sure he passes. There's a big bonus waiting for me when he returns home with all his certificates, and I've already got my new Viper picked out, so don't screw this up."

"But he won't actually know how to fly. He's going to be flying jets with hundreds of passengers on board when he gets home. What happens when one day his automation fails and he has to actually fly the plane for real? He's not going to be able to do it."

"Look, this is the way it works in Third World countries; some rich prince gets the job whether he knows how to do it or not. Why do you think so many crashes happen down there? Look, it's not my job to solve the problems of the world. His dad's paying me to send him home with papers and a logbook that looks legit. Beyond that I don't care. They'll probably give him a copilot that actually knows how to fly. I don't know. Either way not our problem. Just get him the hours he needs, and I'll make sure he takes his checkride with my guy."

"Your guy? What if I don't want to sign him off? I mean I'm not comfortable signing someone off knowing damn well they can't pass a legitimate checkride."

"Oh, don't worry. Ian will sign him off if you don't want to. I just figured you'd maybe want to step up to the plate for once and be a team player. There's long-term benefits in it for you if you do."

"I don't want to be like Ian."

"Well, think about it. There's some multi time in it for you if you change your mind. And I know how much you need multi time."

"I do need multi time, but I don't want to get it like this."

"Just think about it. I could have a lot more opportunities for you in the future, but you've got to be willing to put the company first. This is the real world. Things aren't always by the book. If you want to make it, you've got to be willing to play the game. Or if you don't want to, I can put you back with George and Antonio. It's up to you. Oh, and by the way, I'm working on something here, and I need an email address that can't be linked back to me. You got one I can use?"

I decided to step down from my position as instructor of the month after the first day. Since I gave it up, it defaulted to the runner-up, Ian. Todd took my picture down off the wall in the lobby that hung next to about forty or fifty pictures of Ian and replaced it with yet another picture of Ian. I was back to flying with George and getting no-call no-shows from Antonio.

-8-

Warm Gasoline

It was winter in Florida, which wasn't much of a winter at all, but you wouldn't believe how people freaked out down there if the temperature dropped below sixty degrees. They acted completely insane and had no idea how to handle it.

I woke up to the sound of several alarms going off, which was normal, but noticed it was only 5:45 a.m. Everyone else was waking up too, and we were each starting to take notice that it wasn't our alarm clocks we were hearing.

"Who's got their alarm clock set early?" Dave shouted. "It's only 5:45! I should have gotten fifteen more minutes of sleep. Someone is going to die for this."

But it wasn't any of us. It was the fire alarm in the building, and I could now hear sirens approaching outside. We had to evacuate.

It was 40 degrees out that morning, which was unusually low for this area even in the winter. It turned out that someone in our apartment complex had been trying to warm gasoline up in a pot on the stove in their apartment because they were afraid their car wouldn't start in the cold temperatures. It was in the building across from ours so luckily our building wasn't damaged in the fire. It would have been devastating for us to lose our sleeping bags, lawn chairs, and alarm clocks.

A building with six apartments in it burned to the ground, though. Thankfully, no one was injured. We all had to wait outside while the fire department put out the fire in the building across the way and cleared the area. I could overhear the guy who started the fire being interviewed by a news reporter out in the parking lot.

"I just didn't want to be late to work," the guy explained. "I mean it's never been this cold here before, and I've heard people have trouble starting their cars up north when it gets cold in the winter. I figured if I warmed the gas up a little, I wouldn't have any trouble. I don't know what went wrong. I put the kettle on the stove, set it on low, went to brush my teeth, and when I came back, the kitchen was on fire."

"So, you where heating a pot of gasoline on your stove? And then you were going to pour it into your gas tank on your car?" the news reporter questioned.

"Yes, ma'am. I figured the warm gas would help the car start easier."

"Wow, that's a pretty smart idea, sir. I've never heard of doing that. I may have to give that a try myself because I too had trouble starting my car this morning in these cold temperatures. I wonder how the fire started, though?"

"I don't know. Must have been something wrong with the stove. You know these landlords. They never want to fix anything. I ought to sue this apartment complex for giving me a faulty stove."

"Sounds like you should, and maybe we need to do a segment on *Eye on your Side* about these slumlords around here providing tenants with faulty stoves."

"Yes, ma'am, I think you should. These slumlords need to be exposed!"

"We better be careful on our way to work today." I told Dave. "With these cold temperatures these people are losing their minds down here."

At the airport things were no better. Every plane that was departing Marbella that morning was asking for de-ice. "It will be about a one-hour delay," the ground controller told me when I called up for taxi.

"What? Why?" There were never delays at this airport.

"That's how long it will be before we can get you de-iced for departure, there's a long line ahead of you, and we have limited de-ice equipment."

"We don't need de-ice," I told him. "It's 40 degrees out. It's not even below freezing, and there's not a cloud in the sky. I don't think this is icing conditions."

"Oh, I can't let you go without it," the ground controller said. "I mean, it's never been this cold here before; you'll probably ice up and crash within minutes if you don't."

I felt like I was in the *Twilight Zone*. "Hasn't anyone here ever left Florida before? It gets way colder than this in most places," I informed him. "You all need to calm down. People are setting apartment buildings on fire trying to warm gasoline up. Now we have mandatory de-icing here. It's only 40 degrees! What the hell is going on?"

One thing was for sure; it needed to warm up quick before this whole city spiraled into an apocalypse.

Todd was freaking out now too but for different reasons. "I'm not paying for any de-ice!" he shouted over company frequency. "Everyone needs to come back here and park it till it warms up."

He never wanted to cancel flights. This was a first. No one was flying, and since the instructors had nothing to do, we were actually able to talk Todd into letting us all leave for the day. That was, at least until the weather turned better and everyone regained their sanity.

Most of us instructors were running low on Ramen Noodles, so we decided to use this unexpected free time to go to the supermarket and stock up. We had to go home and change out of our uniforms first because Marbella Flight Academy, as well as most flight schools and airlines, had a policy stating that pilots can't apply for or use food stamps or welfare while in uniform. The aviation industry has a lot of policies in place for the soul purpose of hiding what the industry is really like. They don't want the general public to know that all the pilots who are flying them around are broke and on government assistance. The policy was actually in our company handbook, and it was no wonder why, since we were all going to be using food stamps to get our Ramen Noodles.

Going to the supermarket was a huge mistake, though. With the chaos that was going on today, it was a borderline riot. The news channels had been running twenty-four-hour coverage about the cold snap, brainwashing everyone into thinking the world might be ending and the food supply was about to run out. The store was ransacked, and the lines were a mile long. Everyone had carts full of bread and milk, which must be the survival meal of choice when faced with an imaginary natural disaster. The chaos was worse than it was the last time there was a hurricane here, which was a real disaster.

On the way back to the apartment, cars were driving off the road left and right and slamming into each other, apparently on some sort of imaginary black ice because the roads were perfectly fine. South Florida was normally a dangerous place to drive; today it was out of control. Between the usual elderly people slow-rolling through red lights and now the hypochondriac black ice imaginers pretending to lose control, it was a demolition derby on the roads. Dave was having to swerve and weave around wrecks that were happening all around us the whole way back to the apartment. I was beginning to think that for our own personal safety, we might need to leave the state until the temperature got back up to sixty degrees. I mean, it wasn't safe at home, it wasn't safe on the road, and we couldn't fly. We didn't know what to do.

Dave turned on the boombox radio that was duct taped to the dash in the Camry. We listened as they were reporting breaking news that the A1A southbound was backed up for fifty miles near Miami due to people trying the evacuate to The Keys seeking warmer temperatures.

Thankfully, by afternoon the weather had warmed up, and things had calmed down. Todd called us all back into work, and when we arrived back at the flight school, I was shocked to see Antonio was there waiting for me. I hadn't seen him since the night when the Airworthiness and Registration Certificates from thirty foxtrot alpha went missing.

"I need you to teach me to fly," he said. "At least a little so I can go solo."

"What, wait, you speak English?"

"Yeah, I just pretended I didn't because I didn't really want to have to come out here to learn to fly. I just wanted to hang out in my hotel room and play video games, but my parents are going to be here to visit tomorrow and they're expecting me to take them for a ride in the plane."

"You mean with me, right?"

"No, uh, they think I can take them by myself because I told them I could. I didn't really think they were going to come here. So, I kinda need to be able to take them, or they're going to make me come home because I think they think I'm lying."

"Well you are lying, and that's impossible. You would need your private pilot's license to take passengers, and there's no way you can get your license by tomorrow. There's no way you can even go solo by tomorrow. I can take them for a ride if they want to go for a ride, but you can't. Are you kidding? You've had no flight training at all."

"Well, Todd said I could. I talked to him this morning, and he told me you'd make it happen."

"Wait here," I told him. "I need to go talk to Todd."

When I walked into Todd's office, he was frantically punching numbers into a calculator. A line of coke was laid out on his desk in front of him with a rolled-up dollar bill lying next to it. He looked up from his calculator. "What can I do for you?" he asked, not bothering to try to hide the drugs that he had probably forgotten were in plain sight on the table.

"What's the deal with Antonio?" I asked. "He speaks perfect English, and now he wants to learn to fly by tomorrow? And you told him that's possible?"

"Hey, I was just as surprised as you are. Just get him to the point he can solo by the end of the day. That way when his parents get here tomorrow, he can take them up for a couple trips around the pattern, and they'll let him stay here. He promised me he'd let me up the no-call no-shows to two hours a flight slot instead of thirty minutes if we do this for him." He paused for a second. "The alternative is he goes home, and we lose out on the money."

"You've got to be kidding me. I can't get someone to solo in one day. And even if I did, he still can't take passengers until he gets his private, and there's no way that's happening in one day. It's impossible."

"He doesn't need to get his private, if something happens, we'll just pretend we didn't notice the passengers getting on the plane when he went for a solo flight."

"This is crazy," I told him, "even for you."

"Hey, like always, if you won't endorse him, my man Ian will. I'm starting to think I don't have much use for you, though."

This was always his ultimatum, do something impossible or stupid, or get fired.

I didn't want to get fired, and at this point, all I really need to do was go fly with Antonio for a while, so I told him, "I'll fly with him and teach him what I can. We'll talk after that."

"My man."

"Yeah, whatever," I said. As I walked out the door and decided to add, "Oh, and don't forget to finish your coke."

I figured I'd skip teaching Antonio how to preflight. Part of me was wanting to see if I could teach this kid how to take off, land, and fly the pattern in one afternoon. I began to see it as a challenge. I knew it probably wasn't possible, but if I did pull this off, it would make for a good story later. I decided to skip anything that wasn't going to be necessary to get him up solo quick. If I stuck to the basics, maybe I could teach him to land by tomorrow? That is, as long as nothing went wrong or nothing unusual happened during his solo flight, in which case, with his limited experience, he wouldn't know how to handle it.

I even gave him a real checklist to use, one page that covered everything, not the ridiculous King James Checklist we were supposed to be using with students. I was hoping it would help speed the process.

As we moved along things were going surprisingly smooth. Antonio seemed to be picking up on everything quickly. It was obvious he was already familiar with the controls and, once airborne, he was flying like he'd done it before. Normally on the first lesson, I would be the one actually flying the plane while the student would follow along with me, but Antonio took control right from the start; I wasn't having to help him much at all. "You never took a flight lesson before?" I asked.

"Nope," he told me. "This is my first time in a small plane like this."

As we approached for our first landing, he was on glidepath, holding airspeed, and seemed to know what he was doing. I kept my hands on the yoke expecting to have to land for him, but he did alright. I mean, it wasn't a perfect landing but not bad at all for his first one. As we climbed out after the first touch-and-go, I told him, "You fly pretty good for someone who's never flow before. Are you sure this is your first time taking a lesson?"

Antonio preceded to tell me that he spends most of his time sitting in his hotel room playing flight simulator on his computer.

"But why would you do that when you could be outside flying for real? I mean, all these no-call no-shows, pretending to not know English? You'd have your private by now."

He didn't see my point. "Why would I want to do that when I could fly a plane from my hotel room and not have to bother with going outside?"

I guess it's just his generation. These kids don't want to do anything for real anymore. They all just want to sit in a dark room and live a virtual life on their computer. The only reason he was out here today was because, like me, his parents were not going to understand his wanting to sit inside and play video games for the rest of his life. They suspected that was what he had been doing the whole time he'd been here, since that's all he did at home. If he could pull this off tomorrow, they'd be off his back for a little while, and he could spend a few more months here in his hotel by himself, playing video games. And he might actually pull it off. At least he'd been spending time playing the right game to prepare for this charade.

We continued on with the training, and after a couple hours of pattern work, I felt like he really could do it. This was probably crazy, but when you're in a crazy environment, you start to do crazy things too.

"Taxi back to the ramp for a minute," I told him, "and hand me your logbook and student pilot certificate."

I couldn't believe I was doing it, but I signed Antonio's solo endorsement and instructed him to make three laps around the pattern with three landings then come back. But before letting him go, I handed him his logbook and a book of matches, then gave him the same speech I always gave a student when I was about to send them solo: "Remember, if you crash and you're still conscious, make sure this logbook with my signature in it burns up with the airplane. Good luck."

I stood on the ramp and watched as he taxied out for his first solo. I could hear the tower radio communications on a loudspeaker mounted on the side on the flight school building. Antonio could fly, there was no doubt about that, and his communication with ATC was impressive for his first day. But I was still nervous about how this was going to go. The kid had potential to be a good pilot, but his real-world experience was so limited that if anything went wrong, he probably wasn't going to know what to do.

I watched him take off and followed him through the pattern as he came around to make his first landing. Not bad, I thought, as he touched down with a slight squeak from the mains. Seconds later he was full throttle and, on his way, again. He passed overhead on downwind then came back around again for the second landing. It was pretty decent again. So far everything was going smoothly. He was still alive, and there was no damage to the airplane yet. This kid might actually pull off a solo at a Class D airport after only two hours of instruction.

On his third landing, though, on short final, there was a problem, a big problem. His engine quit. My heart skipped a beat, I could hear the rumble of the engine from where I was standing, and now there was nothing but silence. I held my breath and watched as he glided in dead stick and made a great landing rolling to a stop on the runway. It was the best landing of the three, and he was safe, but he hadn't said anything to ATC about the engine quitting yet.

For a moment I breathed a sigh of relief, but the airport was busier than usual that afternoon, and there were two planes on final approach behind him, the closest being a Citation Jet on five mile final. Over the loudspeaker I could hear the tower controller, "*Five foxtrot alpha, don't stop on the runway. I need you to exit left turn next taxiway. Traffic on final.*" He didn't realize Antonio's engine had quit because Antonio hadn't said anything. A few seconds later, "*Five foxtrot alpha, exit the runway immediately!*"

No response.

Moments later I saw Antonio jump out of the Warrior, hop off the right wing, and run around to the front. He grabbed the prop and began pulling the plane by hand toward the side of the runway.

"Citation two x-ray lima, go around! Aircraft disabled on the runway!" the tower shouted when he saw what Antonio was doing.

The Citation went missed as Antonio dragged the plane into the grass alongside the runway.

The grass was wet and muddy from recent rains, and there was a slight slope downhill away from the runway. Antonio slipped and fell in the wet grass, and the plane kept rolling right over the top of him, the nose gear tire just nearly missing him, as he thrashed around in the mud trying to get back up. The tower controller then instructed the second plane on final to go around too. Once the Warrior came to stop in a low spot at the bottom of the slope, Antonio caught back up to it, jumped up on the right wing, and climbed back inside.

"Five foxtrot alpha, this is Marbella Tower. How do you read?"

After a few moments, he responded, out of breath and in a panic, *"Ah, I'm here. My, ah, engine stopped."*

"Do you need assistance?"

"I think so, ah, yes."

"Copy that. A tug is on its way. Break. Attention, all traffic, Marbella Airport is temporarily closed due to a disabled aircraft in the grass."

When Antonio got back to the ramp, he climbed out of the Warrior that looked like it had been out muddin'. His black leather pants and jacket were also covered in mud.

"What happened?" I asked. "Did it just quit?"

He told me that on his third landing, when he reached to pull the throttle to idle, on short final, he grabbed the mixture instead. He killed the fuel.

"Mistakes happen," I said, "but if that was it, why didn't you just push the mixture back in and restart the engine?"

"Oh, I didn't think of that."

As it turns out, the one thing he didn't get from his video game was any common sense. Maybe sending someone solo after only two hours of training was a mistake. Todd didn't think so. "No big deal," he said. "Just make sure you call the tower and apologize."

"Fine." I said.

"And don't forget to endorse him for his solo flight with his parents tomorrow."

"Fine," I said and turned to leave his office. But Todd had one more thing.

"Oh, and that line of blow was real nice." He pulled a plastic bag out of his desk drawer and held it up. "Got some for you here if you want? Might cheer you up a bit."

"No thanks," I said. "I've gotta get home and throw a pot of gasoline on the stove. It's gonna be cold one tonight."

Antonio's flight the following day with his parents went without a hitch. They were satisfied, and after that I never saw him again. He probably spent the rest of his time in Florida at the Holiday Inn Express playing video games. However, his name was still on my schedule, two flight slots every day, and Todd continued to charge him for two hours of flight training each for the rest of the time I worked there.

-9-
A Day at the Beach

Ian called in sick. This was a frequent occurrence that normally went unnoticed, but today all the instructors were talking about it. Rumor had it that he'd had a seizure the day before in the middle of a simulated single-engine approach in the Seminole. The multi student he was flying with at the time freaked out and then attempted to go missed single engine. The Seminole wouldn't climb on one engine, though, and his attempted missed approach was about to wind up being an NTSB (National Transportation Safety Board) report about controlled flight into terrain.

Luckily, he realized it wasn't going to work fairly quickly, changed his mind about it, and made a quick decision to chop the throttle and put it down just short of running off the end of the runway.

When Ian came to, he begged the student not to tell anyone what had happened, but the rumor was getting around quickly, so he must have told someone with loose lips. Every instructor who heard the news had the same reaction. Epilepsy; this would explain why he couldn't get a legit medical certificate.

Now, this is a terrible condition for someone to have. But acting as a pilot while knowing he had this condition was far worse, especially when he was flying around with student pilots who might not be able to handle the plane while he was incapacitated.

This all became bad news for me when Todd told me I was going to have to endorse one of Ian's students for a solo cross-country that day.

"Is this the same student who was flying the pattern with a tailwind and not speaking to anyone at Coral Island a little while back?" I asked.

"I don't know, probably," he said.

I nodded. "Great!"

The student was a Greek kid named Matthew. He was to be flying a three-leg VFR solo cross-country from Marbella to Pahokee, then onto Port Charlotte, and back to Marbella.

When I found him in the weather briefing room, he had nothing prepared for the flight: no course plotted out, no waypoints, no fuel burn calculations, nothing.

"Aren't you supposed to be leaving in fifteen minutes?" I asked. "Why didn't you prepare for this?"

"I don't need to. I can figure out flight plan on my way there," he responded in broken English and with an attitude.

"No, you need to figure this stuff out ahead of time. You don't even know how much fuel you'll need."

"There's always enough fuel. They fill planes up full before every flight."

"They do, but how do you know a full tank's enough if you haven't even calculated how much it will take? It might take more than a full tank."

"Ian told me it be enough."

"That's fine, but you still need to calculate it for yourself; it's a training exercise. You can't just always assume that there's going to be enough fuel because someone else told you there would be. I want you to tell me how much you need and how much you have, and at least come up with a course to follow so you know what heading to fly to get there."

"Uh, fine. I do. I do." He was obviously annoyed with all this.

"Do it now, and I'll come back in fifteen minutes to check your numbers, but you better be quick because I've got another student to fly with."

"Fine."

Normally, it would take students at this stage in their training at least an hour if not longer to plan out a flight like this, which is why he should have done it the night before. What usually happens, though, is instead of planning their cross-country the night before the student goes out and gets hammered till the bars close, sleeps till the last minute, and then shows up ten minutes before their flight and attempts to whip something up really quickly.

This kid wasn't even wanting to bother at all, though.

I came back fifteen minutes later, and he had a half-ass flight plan scribbled out. I looked it over quickly, and at least his headings were close. I still wasn't too excited about sending someone who had prepared so little, but I knew if I didn't, I would be facing backlash from Todd.

"Alright, this will do," I told him. "Did you file your flight plans with Flight Service?"

"No."

"You need to file a flight plan for each leg."

"Why?"

"So they know you're out there. Once you're airborne, open it with Flight Service over the radio, and after you land at each stop, call to close it from the FBO there when you're on the ground. That way they know to look for you if you never arrive."

"No, thank you, I don't need too. It's OK."

"Yes, you do. Call Flight Service and file them. If you don't know how to, I can help you."

"I know how, but it's not needed. I fly the cross-country; it's fine."

"Yes, it is needed, and it's school policy. And when you land at Pahokee and Port Charlotte, I need you to call into the school here and let us know you made it. Also, I'm going to give you a form to have the FBO at each stop sign. You need to bring back to me."

"Why? I'm fine."

"Because that's the rules. Everyone has to do it when they go solo."

We continued to argue back and forth about this for a few minutes until he finally agreed to file flight plans while I stood there and watched. I knew if I didn't, he wasn't going to do it. When he was ready to go, I reluctantly endorsed his logbook for the flight and sent him on his way.

After that I left with George so we could go up and fly in circles for a couple hours while trying to find Calusa, with no luck. It was another 1.8 in my logbook, and that was all that really mattered to me at this point.

Arriving back at the flight school after my flight with George I checked in with Todd. "Did Matthew call from Pahokee yet?"

"No, haven't heard from him."

"What?" I questioned. "He left two hours ago; he should have been there and on his way to Port Charlotte by now."

"Maybe he forgot to call. I'm sure he's fine."

Todd wasn't concerned; he never was, but I was. I'm the one who signed this wind-ignoring, non-flight planning, non-communicator off for this cross-country, so I was going to be the one answering to the FAA if something went wrong. I decided I better call Flight Service to make sure he closed his flight plan when he landed in Pahokee.

"He never opened it," the guy from Flight Service told me over the phone. "I see here where three flight plans were filed this morning, but none of them have been opened."

"Oh, that son of a bitch. I should have known he'd never bother. Thanks," I said. "I'll call Pahokee Airport and see if they've seen him."

But when I called the Pahokee Airport FBO, they hadn't seen him either. I gave them the tail number and the description of the plane and told them what Matthew looked like.

"Are you sure?" I asked. "A short Greek kid with a bad attitude hasn't been there?"

"No," the guy from the FBO said. "He hasn't been here. I'm sure of it. There's only been a couple planes in this morning, and I've been here since 7 a.m. I would have seen him if he were here."

It was a small airport on Lake Okeechobee with just a trailer for an FBO. There's no way they could have missed him if he had been there. He never made it. He could be lost somewhere, or he could have gone down in the Everglades.

When I informed Todd of this news, his eyes lit up when he asked, "Which plane was he in?"

"Six foxtrot alpha," I told him.

"Oh yeah, good. That plane's a piece. What time did he leave?"

When I told him, he looked at the clock. "He wouldn't have run out of fuel yet. He could still be airborne and lost somewhere. If we don't hear anything after a couple more hours, I'll call the insurance company."

"Why is that the first call you're going to make?"

I was starting to think this flight school was really just a front for some sort of insurance scam. But while Todd was so eager to write Matthew and his plane off, I was concerned for him even if the kid were a pain in the ass. And I was starting to kick myself for letting him go with so little preparation.

I called Flight Service back to let them know the plane had never reached its destination and that it was missing. They told me they would check with ATC facilities along his route to see if anyone had spoken to him or seen him on their radar. However, he let me know it was a long shot because there were tons of planes out there buzzing around VFR, squawking twelve-hundred, in uncontrolled airspace, and probably no one would have taken notice of him if he did cross their radar screen.

A couple hours passed by slowly while I sat around waiting for news, but nothing came. It was one of my two flight slots that Antonio was penciled into, and while Todd was cashing in on Antonio's no-call no-show I had nothing else to do except sit around and wait.

In the meantime, Dave came back early from his flight because they'd had, yet again, another radio problem.

"I want to see the maintenance log," he demanded of Todd. "Show me where a mechanic signed it off that it's fixed. I've told you about radio problems in this plane three times now, and nothing's getting done about it. The tower is getting pissed. This is the third time in two days I had to squawk 7600 and land-lost coms using light gun signals."

"Don't worry, I'm writing it up in the maintenance log," Todd said. "I'll take the plane down to maintenance and tell them to work on it again."

"I don't believe your even taking it down there." Dave shot back. "You probably just taxi down to the other end of the airport, park it for an hour, and then bring it back without ever doing anything. I don't understand why the instructors can't write stuff up themselves like every other flight school."

Dave had a point. Todd kept the maintenance logs for all the planes in his office where we couldn't see them. If we had a problem with a plane, we had to go to him and ask him to write it up. We weren't allowed to do it ourselves, and we were all sure that he never did.

He would tell us he was taking the plane to maintenance then taxi off across the field in it. He would always be back after a while claiming it was fixed, but we never saw any paperwork showing what or if anything at all had been done to resolve the problem. It was common to have the exact same problem again right after it had supposedly been fixed.

Todd would try to switch the planes around between instructors after there had been a complaint about one of them, probably in the hopes that the next person to take it would be unaware of the issue until they were already airborne and would maybe just put up with whatever was wrong with it for the remainder of the flight. Then if that instructor complained, Todd would pass the plane on to a different instructor, and so on. He'd sometimes get away with not fixing a plane for three days with this tactic. We had caught on, though. At this point everyone knew that if Todd asked one of us to switch to another plane at the last minute, we should start asking around to the other instructors to see if anyone knew what was wrong with it.

"Here, I'll get you another plane since you're whining about it," Todd told Dave. "Why don't you take this one?" He handed him a clipboard.

Dave was satisfied and left with his student, and Todd taxied off in the plane with the radio problems, supposedly taking it to some maintenance facility none of us were sure even existed.

For now, my entertainment was over. I made a phone call to Port Charlotte Airport to see if Matthew had been there since by this time he should have been there too and on his way back here by now, but they hadn't seen him either. I left my number and told them to call if he showed up.

It had reached the point where if he'd been airborne this whole time, he would have been long since out of gas. Still nothing from Flight Service, though, and if a plane crash had been reported somewhere, they would know about it, which gave me hope that the kid was still alright.

After Todd returned from his maintenance run, he was practically counting his winnings when I told him that Matthew never made it to Port Charlotte either. He promptly snatched up one of the papers that had been taped to his wall and said, "See it's a good thing I hadn't been making the payments on six foxtrot alpha. What a waste that would have been. They can't repo it now."

"Are you making the payments on any of the planes?" I asked.

"No, I let them all fall behind. When they start threatening repossession then I make a payment to get them off my back for a little while. In general, I like to stay about a 120 days delinquent on everything. Helps with cash flow."

"Hell of a way to run a business," I told him.

George showed up to fly his afternoon flight slot, and I contemplated canceling with him. I really wasn't in the mood to fly, especially not with him. At the moment I was afraid I had too much on my mind to stay focused on keeping him from killing us. Todd and Ian may have been able to have no conscience about a student going missing, but I wasn't them. Sitting here and staring at the clock waiting for news wasn't helping, though, and George was as eager as ever to fly so I figured at least I wouldn't let him down.

While George preflighted, I told him about Matthew being missing. I figured at least it could be a lesson for him on why it's important to not only file but to also open your flight plan. Not that he'd ever be in a position to where he'd need to. I didn't envision him making any solo cross country's anytime soon or ever for that matter.

"Don't worry, sir," George said. "I'd always file a flight plan. I'm not like Matthew. He's dangerous. I told him, I don't like you cause you're dangerous."

"Yeah, he's dangerous," I said. "Still, I hope he makes it back here. I don't really want to be named instructor of the month again."

After returning from the flight with George, there was still no news. Todd told me that Flight Service had called while I was gone, and they still hadn't been able to locate Matthew.

I waited around the rest of the day; even after all the other instructors piled into the Camry to head home, I stayed. It was just Todd and me here waiting, and finally at six p.m., an hour after the flight school closed, the phone rang.

I answered. "Hello?"

It was Marbella Tower, "Hey, your guy just checked in ten miles out."

"You're kidding."

"I'm serious. He's not acting like anything is wrong. So, I'm not going to say anything to him about anyone missing him because I don't want to make him nervous. I'll let you handle it when he gets there."

"Thanks," I said. "That's great news. We'll be waiting for him here."

But while I was happy to hear Matthew was OK, Todd was pissed, "Well, I guess I need to cancel my insurance claim."

"Don't worry," I told him. "Ian will be back soon. You'll have plenty of insurance claims in your future."

Several minutes later Matthew taxied onto the ramp and parked the plane. Todd and I watched him through the window as he tied the plane down and gathered his stuff.

My mood had changed from concerned for his safety to angry about where he had been for the last ten hours. There's no way he could have been airborne this entire time; he had to have gone somewhere, and even if he had legitimately gotten lost and ended up somewhere else, at the very least he could have called.

"You want tell us where you've been all day?" I asked him when he walked in the door.

Matthews froze in his tracks when he saw us standing there. "Uh, I did cross-county. Ah, Pahokee, ah, Port Charlotte."

"Bullshit," I said. "You were never at either place. We've been looking for you for hours. Where did you go, and why didn't you call?"

"I was there. I went to Pahokee and Charlotte. Look, I have paper you gave me to have people there sign." He began fishing in his bag, trying to find the form that I'm sure he forged.

"I don't need to see it," I said, "I've called both places several times. We already know you were never there. I've been looking for you all day and so has Flight Service. You never opened your flight plans like you were supposed to."

"I did too. I called like you told me."

"No, you didn't! Tell us where you really went!"

He didn't respond.

"Matthew, where did you go?" I asked again.

Todd finally spoke up "Come on," he said. "Just tell us." Though when he said it, he seemed more irritated by the whole conversation at this point than he seemed upset about a student disappearing.

"Matthew, we know you didn't fly the cross country. Where did you go?"

He stood for a few moments staring at me, his eyes glazed in anger. He knew he was caught but he wasn't sorry about it, he became defensive. "Who cares where I've been? I brought plane back. I was gone a while, so what."

"Just tell us where you went," Todd said in an exhausted tone.

Matthew then finally admitted, "I have friend that's in Venice, at flight school there. I go there to eat lunch and see him a while. Then we go to beach. I was going to come back, but I lose track of time. No big deal."

"Man, we thought you were dead all day," I told him. "You can't just disappear with an airplane. When you get your license, which now I'm not sure you'll ever get, you can rent a plane and go anywhere you want, but as a student pilot going solo you can only go exactly where I told you to go. And we need to know where you are at all times."

"I don't see why such a big deal," Matthew said.

"Well, it is a big deal." I looked at Todd. "What do you want to do?" I asked. I figured he'd be as upset as I was about all this, but he wasn't; he didn't care at all. If he wasn't making any insurance claims today, he was no longer interested.

"Well, I think he's learned his lesson," Todd said. "Matthew, have a good night; we'll see you tomorrow."

What a waste of time caring, I thought as he picked up his flight bag and gave me a smirk that said, "I win."

After Matthew walked out the door I said to Todd, "Nothing? He stole your plane for a whole day. I would think you'd be upset about it. After all this, no punishment?"

"Hey, he's the customer. He the one paying. It wouldn't do me any good suspending him. I want him back here tomorrow flying. He's still got money in his account."

This was a huge difference between this place and where I went to school. I learned to fly at a public university where a stunt like this would have without question resulted in the student being kicked out of the program. At Todd's flight school, however, it was a private business. And at a private business, the customer is always right. Meaning it was the students making the rules and running the show here. Not the instructors and not even Todd.

Alex Stone

-10-

The Real Maverick

Over the next few months the flight school had a terrible string of bad luck. First Todd's paper shredder caught fire and nearly burned the building down. Luckily, the airport fire department responded quickly before the fire spread far beyond his office, and the building was repairable. All of his important documentation that had been in there was lost to fire, though, leaving him unsure of how far past due he was on all of his bills.

Shortly thereafter one of the planes was repossessed since he had forgotten to make a payment on it before it went more than 120 days past due. After that happened, he quickly decided to pay all his bills current to avoid this happening a second time, that is, until he could get his office repaired and reorganize his well-oiled system of constant delinquency.

This put a big squeeze on his cash flow, so he informed all the instructors that our paychecks had been lost in the fire as well and could not be recovered.

"Can't you just get a new checkbook and write us all new paychecks?" we asked. It seemed reasonable considering it was the checks that were lost and not the actual money.

However, "No," was his answer. They were apparently irreplaceable. We would just not be paid for that two-week period.

This left the instructor group even more disgruntled than normal. In retaliation, one of us, and I'm not sure who, decided to blow the whistle on the flight school and call the JAA (Joint Aviation Authority) to inform them that instructors here had been training students for the purposes of obtaining European JAA PPL licenses (the European equivalent of a private pilot's license) without having the proper credentials to do so.

Students coming to the school to earn European licenses had been a big business for Todd; it was almost half the students. The problem was that only one instructor who worked here had the proper certification to train these students, and he couldn't possibly handle all of them by himself.

Todd had been telling us all for months he was going to send more of us to take the four-hour course to get certified, but he never did because he didn't want to spend the three hundred bucks on it. Instead of getting more of us certified for it, Todd would force uncertified instructors do the actual flight training with most of these students, then have the one instructor who was certified signing their logbooks. So, on paper it looked like he was the one doing all the flight training as well as endorsing them for checkrides.

On a random Wednesday morning, the JAA raided the flight school like a swat team. Armed with M-16s, they kicked in the doors and busted through the windows. When they found Todd, they held him at gunpoint and demanded to see all the students flight training records and logbooks. Begrudgingly, he turned them over, and the end result was Todd lost the school's credentials to teach any JAA students for life. All of those students that were here seeking European licenses were forced to leave and go elsewhere for training, leaving us with half the students we had before.

Todd promptly began a witch hunt amongst the instructor group, which resulted in four instructors being fired for being the suspected whistle blower, though he was never able to determine for sure who was responsible. None of us were either; whoever did it never told a soul.

Now with the student count cut in half, Todd was frantically trying to get new students into the school, and he was finding people, but the quality was even lower than normal.

I was supposed to get a new student one day, but he never showed up. I found out later that afternoon that he had been pulled over and arrested for DUI while on his way to the airport for his very first flight lesson. He later bailed out of jail and did show up the next day to fly, drunk again, of course. He let me know that that day he'd gotten a ride to the airport for his flight lesson, since he had decided he was way too drunk to drive here. He seemed harmless, though, and I didn't have anyone else to fly with, so I took him up anyway. He passed out a couple minutes into the flight. It was a nice smooth day, and the rumble of the engine put him right to sleep. I needed the flight time and the money, so I just flew around with him sleeping in the seat next to me for a couple hours. He was paying for the flight. I figured if this is how he wanted to spend his money, sleeping through a flight lesson, well that's his journey.

He actually turned out to be one of my favorite students. I didn't have to teach him anything or keep him from killing us. He would just go to sleep, and I could spend a couple hours actually getting to fly around myself. The only problem was, I had to put up with his whiskey sweat smell, but fortunately for me the exhaust fumes leaking into to the cockpit helped mask it. At the end of each flight once I parked us back on the ramp, I'd wake him up, and he'd call his ride to come drive him back to the bar where he'd hang out for a few hours till his next flight slot.

The bad luck streak continued, though. After my flight with George one day, he borrowed another student's Ducati and attempted to recreate a scene from *Top Gun*, riding alongside the runway on the airport access road while a plane was taking off. It was his first time on a motorcycle, though, and he was about as good a rider as he was a pilot. He took off and ripped through three gears before he missed a turn, dumped it, and went rolling through the grass.

A bunch of us had been standing outside watching this nonsense, and when we saw him go down, we ran to help him.

"You alright, George?" I asked when we got to him.

He was laying in the grass, holding his leg in pain, and didn't respond right away.

"George, you alright? You can't die on me, I won't have any students left."

"Yeah, I'm alright," he said. "I just hit my knee pretty hard when I got thrown off. How did it look, though? Did it look awesome?"

"Yeah, man, you looked pretty cool until you wrecked. For a second there, right before you went over the handle bars, I thought you were the real Maverick."

"Sweet."

"Here, Dave's gonna take you to the hospital to get checked out."

"OK."

We loaded George up in the back of the Camry, and Dave drove him to the emergency room. He didn't have any broken bones, just bruises; he was going to be fine. The doctor told him he needed to take it easy for a couple weeks, though, and that meant no flight training.

Until he got better, I was down another student.

And the streak wasn't over. Things got worse on the way back from the hospital. Dave got pulled over for having a daytime running light out on the Camry. This wasn't the first time he'd been pulled over and hassled for something ridiculous in Marbella. The last couple times he was able to talk his way out of it by claiming he was a tourist here on vacation. The police never hassle tourists no matter how shitty their car is, but I think they had seen his car around town enough over the past few months to know that wasn't the truth. And if he lived here, the real problem was that he wasn't driving a Cadillac or a Town Car. The

Camry just didn't fit in down here, and it really didn't help matters when Dave tried to make a joke of the traffic stop.

"Do you know why I pulled you over?" the officer asked him.

"Cause I'm all jacked up on PCP?" Dave responded.

"What?"

"Sorry, I'm just joking, man. I didn't take any PCP today. I'm a pilot, and I was just bringing this guy to the hospital because he dumped a Ducati trying to recreate a scene from *Top Gun*."

"Sir, can I see your license and registration please?"

"Of course, Officer. Let me get those for you."

Dave fished around in the center console for a minute and while he did the cop asked, "So, how long have you been living in Florida?"

Dave paused for a moment, he thought about lying again but then thought different. It was time for him to come clean. "Oh, I've been living here about eight or nine months, Officer." He then pulled out the documents and handed them out the window.

The cop examined the registration for a moment, then walked around to the back of the car to look at the license plate. When he came back, he said, "Sir, this doesn't match your plates. And your driver's license is from a different state too. You're supposed to register your vehicle and get a Florida license within thirty days after moving into the state."

"Oh, God damn it," Dave said. "I told my secretary to take care of that. She probably never did it, that bitch. You know, it's hard to find good help these days."

The cop stepped back a second and looked at Dave's car again. Surely thinking anyone that drove this car did not have a secretary. "Your secretary?" he questioned.

"Yeah, I'm going to have to fire her now. I'm sorry about this, Officer. I'll get it taken care of ASAP."

"Wait here a minute," he told Dave.

He went back to his cruiser for a few minutes. When he returned, he told Dave, "I'm going to give you twenty-four hours to get your car registered in Florida, and you need to get a Florida license with your current address on it too. Once you do that, you need to come down to the station and show us. As long as you to that by tomorrow, you won't get a ticket. But if you don't, I'm going to put an APB out on this car. Understand?"

"Yes sir, I understand. It won't happen again."

He handed Dave his paperwork back, and before he walked away added, "And go easy on your secretary."

Dave drove away, but he had no plans of registering the car. He was close to reaching one thousand hours and would probably be leaving the state soon anyway. Pilots move so often, it was too much of a hassle to change everything over every time we were living in a new state. Most of us had a license from somewhere we lived four or five states ago. Plus, since he never got his last paycheck, he had no money for a new registration anyway. Twenty-four hours later, the Camry would now officially be on the Marbella police radar.

-11-
Biennial Flight Review

Better news came the next day when Todd told me he had a biennial flight review for me to do. "Some old timer I met at the supermarket. He's already outside. Should be easy. Here you go," he said and handed me the clipboard for the plane.

Biennial flight reviews were a requirement for people who have a pilots' license to stay current if they were not employed as a pilot. Most of the time, it was weekend warriors who came in for these, people who weren't professional pilots but had a license and flew for fun on the weekends. A lot of them down there were rich doctors that own their own planes and used it to fly themselves and their families around on weekend trips. This guy was different, though.

I met him out on the ramp where he was already preflighting the plane, and he told me his name was Clarence. He looked like he was about eighty years old and seemed to know what he was doing. I asked to see his logbook, and he handed me an old leather-bound journal that looked like something that had been recovered from a bombed-out building in France after the war. I flipped through the delicate pages that were filled with an old-time form of cursive that appeared to have been written with a quill. I couldn't read any of it, but when I flipped to the back, I found that toward the end there was modern flight logs in there from other instructors in recent years.

I saw that the last time he had flown was his last flight review a couple years ago and the last flight before that was a flight review four years ago and so on. It seemed as though he didn't really use his license anymore but was still keeping it current just so he had it.

After speaking with him for a few minutes, he seemed like a sweet old man, and I figured this was going to be a nice easy flight: go up, do a few maneuvers, practice a few landings, sign the guy off for a couple more years, and done. He'd probably fly about the same speed as most people drove around here, slow and steady.

Boy was I wrong. This old man was about to take me for the ride of my life.

Everything was pretty calm until we took the runway. But as soon as we did, he slammed the throttle forward so hard I'm surprised he didn't shatter every bone in his eighty-year-old hand. At rotation speed he ripped the plane off the deck like we had reached the end of the aircraft carrier and our only option was either going up or going off the end of the boat into the ocean. It was then I realized, in his mind, we were at war.

"Six foxtrot alpha left turn toward the practice area at your discretion," the tower told us just moments into the climb. A second later, Clarence jerked the plane into a seventy-degree left bank and buzzed by the tower as we headed out to practice some maneuvers on a nice Saturday afternoon.

The way this guy was flying was crazy aggressive, and normally with any other student I'd say something right away. I probably would have even taken the controls by now if this were anyone else, but this was a situation I'd never been in before. This guy was more than three times my age and probably years ago he had flown in stuff far worse than what I had ever seen. It just felt like it would be wrong for me to try and correct him. Usually my students were younger than me. I'd had some that were older before, but not this much older. It would be like trying to school your grandparents on the ways of the world.

I kept quiet, held on tight, and didn't say a word about the way he was flying. He knew what he was doing, and when we got out to the practice area, he was able to perform all the maneuvers just fine. There was really nothing to critique him on except, be a little gentler.

"Nobody is trying to shoot us down," was what I wanted to say, but I didn't say it. I just held on and hoped there were no frays in the flight control cables that might give out or cracks in the wing spars that wanted to get bigger. We were pushing the design envelope of this old trainer in every direction possible, and structural failure was seeming like a real possibility.

His steep turns were as aggressive as his turn out after we rotated. I'm pretty sure we pulled at least four Gs. I cut him off after a hundred and eighty degrees and said, "That's good. You don't have to go all the way around."

I had planned to have him demonstrate a couple stalls and recoveries next, but I was a little nervous about anything where the throttle would be jockeyed around more than it had to be, especially after the incident awhile back with George. I really wasn't interested in the thought of having to put this plane down with either the throttle stuck at full power or at idle again.

"Looks like you've got the maneuvers down pretty well," I told him. "How about we go do a couple touch-and-goes at Calusa?"

"Fine by me," he said and immediately cranked us into a hard-left bank toward the north.

The flight had to be at least one hour on the Hobbs to satisfy the requirement for the biennial review. My thoughts at this point were how we could kill an hour with as little maneuvering as possible but without tipping this guy off to the fact that I was trying to get this over with while doing as little as possible. Coral Island was closer to us than Calusa, and we could have gone there, and he would have been able to get more landings in, but that's exactly what I was trying to avoid. I was hoping by the time we'd get to Calusa and do one landing, we could head back to Marbella and be done.

I still hadn't seen him land yet, though, and was nervous about what was in store for me.

We flew all the way to Calusa at full throttle, and he chose not to fly the pattern when we got there. Straight in on final, chop the power, and dive: that's the only way to do it when the Nazis are chasing you down.

He was on a glidepath that was going to work, so again, I let him do it. When we got down to the runway, he flared and held it there a second. *This might not be bad*, I thought. Then—*slam*, he pushed the nose forward, planted it on all three wheels, and immediately hit the brakes so hard I had to grab the glareshield to keep from losing any teeth. Every loose item in the plane came flying forward.

We came to a full stop; he hit the flap lever and then wham, full throttle.

Normally I was watching the Hobbs meter tick during training flights, adding up in my head how much flight time was going into my logbook. Today I didn't care if I even got to log this time. It just needed to get to one hour quickly, and I wasn't sure if this plane could even take a full hour of this abuse.

On the climb-out, I realized that this one landing hadn't killed enough time. We had gotten here so quickly and with the straight in approach, we couldn't go back to Marbella yet.

"Let's do one more." I told him. "This time you don't need to come to a complete stop, though. Just retract the flaps while we're rolling and take off again." I figured this might be a little easier on the plane and potentially save me on some dental expenses since Todd did not provide the instructors with health insurance, or any other benefits for that matter.

"Sure thing, partner," he said and immediately ripped us into a hard-left bank at just 300 AGL. We were abeam the numbers in seconds, at which point he chopped the throttle and turned a short base leg that curved right into final.

The second landing was the same, but at least he didn't hit the brakes this time. He flipped the flap lever up, and we were off.

"That's good. You can head back to Marbella now." I told him. *One more*, I told myself as I watched the Hobbs meter tick.

On short final into Marbella, the stall horn was sounding as we passed over the approach lights. Clarence put it down right on the threshold and was immediately on the brakes again, hard. We made the first taxiway, which was something I'd never seen done before. I have to admit it was impressive, though it wasn't going to help us get to 1.0 on the Hobbs. I had been hoping for a longer taxi.

We were on the ramp within seconds, and when we pulled into our parking spot, the Hobbs meter was showing point-nine. It was just short, and I was about to say, "Ah, we need to sit here and let it run for six minutes." *Screw it*, I thought. *I'm putting 1.0 in his logbook anyway.*

"Go ahead and shut it down," I told him.

"Where'd you learn to fly?" I asked as we walked into the flight school.

"On Lake Michigan," he told me. "They turned boats into aircraft carriers for training up there during the war."

"Yeah, that's what I figured."

When I filled out and signed his logbook, I felt like I should have left a warning in there for the next instructor that Clarence would fly with. But I didn't know how to do it without his noticing. Instead I wrote, "Nice short field landings." I guess two years from now the next instructor to give him a biennial review will be just as surprised as I was.

The very next flight slot, Matthew took that same plane that Clarence and I had just flown up solo. He flew it down to Coral Island to practice some landings in preparation for his upcoming checkride.

On his first touch-and-go there, right after touching down, one of the main gear wheels fell off. He skidded to a stop on the runway with the right main landing gear strut grinding into the pavement. The wheel rolled off the side of the runway, through the grass, and into the swamp with the gators.

He called into the flight school, in a panic, to tell me that the plane was disabled on the runway and that the Coral Island Airport Authority was losing patience with him quickly over their only runway being closed.

"They said they've got a jet coming in with some important person on it," he told me over the phone. "If I don't find a way to get the plane moved quickly, they said they're going to plow it off the side of the runway with a bulldozer and shove it into the swamp. You've got to help me."

"Who is this?" I said. "I think you have the wrong number."

I guess karma would come back around for him after all.

-12-
Discovery Flight

"DON'T MOLEST THE ALLIGATORS," the sign next to the pond at our apartment complex read, and Dave was furious about it.

"What kind of sick fucks are molesting these alligators?!" He fumed.

"I think they just mean not to mess with them." I tried to calm him down. "I don't think anybody is actually molesting them in the way you're thinking."

"Oh, I know what these people are like down here. I swear to god if I see someone out here diddling an alligator, I'll rip their arms off! Sick bastards, into that weird shit!"

"Don't worry," I assured him, "I think the alligators would rip their arms off first. They'll be fine. They can protect themselves."

We had some rare time off and were trying to fish in the pond, but we weren't catching anything, and trying to keep Dave calm was more stressful than work at this point.

Dave had 992.6 hours of flight time. He was almost at the end of his instructing days, and it was starting to show. He had been here too long, and he was so close to the end he could barely take it anymore.

New instructors would show up down here bright eyed and bushy tailed, but after a few months of putting up with these students and all Todd's shit they were left broken, bitter, and angry. That's where Dave was at: bitter, angry, and ready to be done with it.

"How did that interview go?" I asked, trying to change the subject. Dave had interviewed the night before at cargo airline in Ohio called Checkflight. It was an overnight cargo operation flying checks from bank to bank, and pilot interviews were conducted in the middle of the night. I guess so they could see if you are capable of staying up late?

"It went well, I think," Dave said. "All they really wanted me to do was explain how I could tell if the gear was 'DOWN AND LOCKED.'"

"That's it?"

"Yeah, they must have a lot of gear up landings or something. Anyway, they picked me up in Ft. Lauderdale on one of their cargo runs, flew me up to Ohio for the interview, and then flew me back in the morning. I think I'm going to take the job if they offer it. Get the hell out of here. You should interview with them."

"Maybe I will. What were the planes like?"

"Oh, they were old, mostly Navajos. They aren't any nicer than what we have here, but at least it's all multi, and I'm not gonna be flying with student pilots anymore."

"Are you going to put in your two weeks with Todd? I asked.

"No," Dave said firmly, and then chuckled. "Two-week notice; he'll notice when I don't show up for work. Fuck that guy."

"Do you think Todd knows you interviewed?" I asked. "Todd has been known to fire instructors on the spot if they even ask for time off to go to an interview somewhere else."

"No, I don't think he knows. I told him my car got impounded yesterday while I was at work, which it did, and I needed to leave early to go get it from the impound lot."

"So, the Marbella Police finally seized the Camry, huh?"

"Yeah, I never got the registration changed, so I figured it was only a matter of time. I was hoping I'd get away with it till I was done here and out of the state. But apparently someone called the police yesterday complaining about a junker parked in the airport parking lot. You know how these rich people freak out if they see a hooptie parked next to their Cadillac."

"So, did you pick it up from impound?"

"Hell no. They wanted $300 to give it back to me. That's more than the car's worth. I figured I was better off buying a new car, so I bought myself a Cadillac."

"What?"

"Yeah, figured I won't get hassled by the cops anymore if I blend in with the locals."

"But how did you afford a Cadillac?"

"Oh, it was only $500."

"A Cadillac for five hundred? That's cheap for a Cadillac, but that's still an expensive car for a pilot. Where did you get five hundred bucks?"

"Oh, I blackmailed Ian, got him to pay for it. I told him I'd call the FAA and tell them about his seizures if he didn't buy me a car."

"Huh? Good idea. So, tell me about this Cadillac."

"Oh man, it's baller. It's an '82 Fleetwood Brougham with only 4,000 miles on it, fully loaded. You wouldn't believe all the used Cadillacs for sale around here with hardly any miles on them. These old people buy them and don't drive them anywhere. They just sit in garages for years and years till someone dies, and then they auction them off at estate sales."

"Nice. Well, let's go for a ride."

The next morning the instructor crew rolled into the Marbella Airport in style, no longer smashed into a tiny Camry. We were now rolling a mint-condition land yacht, five instructors across each bench seat and two in the trunk. Blue with a blue vinyl top, leather seats: this thing was fully loaded. It had air conditioning and a tape deck.

But it would be short lived. Dave found out that morning this would be his last day as an instructor. He got the job at Checkflight, and the rest of us were soon to be without a ride to work.

His final day as an instructor would not go smoothly, though. It seemed like when any instructor was finally at the point of seeing the light at the end of the tunnel, their luck changed from bad to worse. Or maybe Todd knew Dave was almost done here and planned a nice send-off.

That day Todd assigned Dave to do a discovery flight. Discovery flights are for people who think they might want to take flight training but aren't sure yet because they've never been in a small training airplane before. The idea was just to fly them around for an hour or so, show them what it's like, let them take the controls a little, and try to get them interested enough to sign up for flight school.

Todd put coupons in the local paper for discounts on discovery flights to draw people in. When they showed up with the coupon, he would just jack up the price of the flight to make up for the discount, though. People thought they were getting a deal; they weren't.

Usually with younger people these flights went well. Teenagers and people in their early twenties weren't afraid and could get excited about the thought of flying a small airplane around. Sometimes, though, we had older people who would come out to do this because they'd been afraid to fly their whole life, and they thought learning to fly, or at least taking a few lessons, was going to help them conquer their fear.

This rarely worked. If someone were afraid to ride on a passenger jet, they are not going to be comfortable in a rickety-ass 1970s two-seater Cessna with one engine and a propeller that leaked oil all over the ramp and reeked of AVGAS inside the cabin.

And that was the case on this particular day for Dave. This guy taking the discovery flight was a lawyer who lived in Coral Island. He obviously was unaware of Marbella Flight Academy's reputation for losing students in the ocean and writing off airplanes, or he wouldn't have been there. He was well off, used to luxury cars, and had flown on private business jets; if he flew commercial, it was first class.

Today he was going to take a ride in an absolute piece of garbage.

The guy seemed nervous from the start, especially once he saw the plane up close. I don't think it was what he was expecting, but he decided to go through with it anyway. He told Dave he wanted to fly over his house and take pictures. That was usually standard procedure on these flights. Everyone wanted to fly over their house, and if there were any celebrities that lived in the area, they wanted to fly over their house too so they could go home and brag to their friends that they flew over so-and-so's house.

Dave decided that he was going to fly him down along the coast first, toward Coral Island.

During the whole time Dave was preflighting, running up the plane, and taxiing out, the guy wouldn't shut up. He went on and on, bragging about his lavish lifestyle and all the high-dollar hookers he banged in Vegas. Once airborne and within minutes into the flight, Dave noticed the guy had gotten quiet, and he was starting to look ill.

"Are you alright?" Dave asked him several times.

"I'm fine," he kept saying, but he was pouring sweat and turning green. Dave fished in the back-seat pocket and found an airsick bag, handed it to him, and told him to just hold on to it. The guy took it and held it in his lap.

There was light chop that day, and people who don't fly much usually don't handle any turbulence well, especially if they're not used to flying in a small plane. This guy was clutching the armrests with every little bump.

"We can go back if you're not feeling well," Dave suggested.

But the guy kept insisting he was fine as they flew farther south from the airport.

Then fifteen minutes into the flight he finally admitted what Dave already knew: "I don't feel so good. I think maybe we should go back."

"No problem. Let me call the tower," Dave told him as he banked left back toward the airport and keyed up the mic. "Marbella Tower this is—"

The guy interrupted: "I don't feel so—*splat!*

The guy lost his spicy tuna roll all over the instrument panel.

He then frantically tried to open the airsick bag but couldn't get it open, throwing up again in his lap and all over the floor.

Dave dove the plane full throttle toward the airport. "Marbella Tower, we're going to need priority handling into the field. I've got a sick passenger."

"Dude, try to get it in the bag if you can," Dave then suggested. In this little plane there was no escaping the smell, and Dave was beginning to worry he was going to get sick himself.

The guy fumbled with the bag as he started heaving again, but in his panic, couldn't get it open. He quickly reached and pulled the latch for the storm window, opening it. Dave tried to stop him yelling, "No!" But it was too late. He went to throw up out the window but the rush of the nearly 100-mile-per-hour wind blew everything back in, covering Dave and splattering all over the inside of the cabin.

He was done after that.

A minute or so later he casually closed the storm window and sat quietly staring at his puke-covered Prada shoes while Dave landed.

"So, tell me again about those prostitutes in Vegas," Dave said as they taxied in, but the guy never replied.

When they parked the plane, the guy quickly got out and left, never to be seen again.

Dave and the entire inside of the Cessna were covered in vomit. Todd demanded Dave clean the plane. That was his policy. "If someone gets sick in your plane, you have to clean it," he told him, embarrassing him in front of other instructors and students.

But Dave was done. He stripped his puke-covered clothes off down to his boxers right in the middle of the lobby in front of everyone, tossing them into a pile on the floor, and stormed out the door.

Alex Stone

The tires squealed as the Fleetwood pealed out of the parking lot, and like that Dave was gone. He was on his way to Ohio to work for Checkflight, taking his Cadillac, our only ride to work, with him.

-13-
Worst Nightmare

Later that afternoon someone else walked into the flight school with a coupon for a discovery flight. It seemed as though Todd's newspaper ad was paying off for him since this was the second walk in today. This guy was strange, though. He caught my attention right away because he was dressed like either some sort of militia member, or he might possibly have been a real-life G.I. Joe character. I'm not sure.

He was wearing camo pants, combat boots, a marron turtleneck, and an army helmet. It looked like he bought all his clothing at a US Army surplus store. That is, except the turtleneck. I'm not even sure where you buy those.

As if he weren't enough on his own, he brought his son with him, who was probably four or five years old and was dressed identically, army helmet and all. The icing on the cake was that Dad had a real mustache, so he put a fake glue on mustache on the kid, making him look like a miniature version of himself.

Todd called me over to the front desk where they were standing. "Lenny here is interested in taking a discovery flight," he told me. "You're not busy. Why don't you take him up?"

"Ah, sure," I said. *What the hell am I getting into here?*

"Great," he said and introduced us. "Lenny, this will be your instructor."

"Hi, Lenny. Nice to meet you." I said, while attempting to shake his hand.

But he didn't shake hands. He and the kid both promptly snapped to attention and shouted, "Nice to meet you instructor, sir!" while saluting me.

"At ease, soldiers," Todd chuckled, obviously getting a kick out it.

After speaking to Lenny for a few minutes I was pretty sure he was a little slow. That's the nicest way to put it. He kept responding to me like we were in the military, but then at times would start giggling at things that weren't funny. He seemed to have the mindset of a child, possibly multiple personalities, and I was almost positive he and his son were both at the same reading level.

I wasn't so sure he was going to be able to process everything that would be necessary to learn how to fly a plane, but what was worse was that he seemed to have a flimsy grasp on reality. He seemed to be under the impression that we would be flying some type of fighter jet today and would be involved in a dogfight with the Russians. He even asked what type of artillery we would have on board and if he could review the "mission plan."

"Excuse me a minute, Lenny," I said. "I'll be right back." I turned to Todd. "Can I talk to you about those maintenance logs really quick? In your office?"

Todd stood up from his seat behind the counter, "Sure," he said, sounding annoyed by it. "Lenny, we'll be right back."

"What's the problem now?" he asked once we were in his office.

"What do you mean what's the problem? That guy is the reason they put locks on the flight deck door on commercial flights."

"Oh, I'm sure he's harmless."

"You don't know that. We haven't done any kind of background screening on him. He could be a serial killer for all we know. He's delusional."

The truth was we didn't know anything about this guy, or any of the other students for that matter. Anyone could show up here for a flight lesson and minutes later be behind the controls of an airplane. There was no screening process whatsoever.

"Oh, I doubt he's a serial killer. I mean, he might be, but I doubt it. I'll tell you what, either you can take him up, or I can get Ian to take him up, and you're fired. Which sounds better?"

Of course, these were my only options. "Oh, I'll take him up. God damn it. But I sure don't have any high expectations for this. He's going to be real disappointed when he finds out we're not going on a bombing run."

After I returned to the lobby, Lenny informed me that his son, Lenny Jr., went everywhere with him and that he would be riding along in the backseat during the flight. I let him know that was no problem, but they would both have to take their army helmets off so they could wear headsets in the plane. That way we could communicate with each other.

At first Lenny had serious concerns about possible head injuries that he might sustain without his helmet during the flight, but I was able to reassure him that all would be OK.

I let him know that I actually never wore a helmet on training flights, and I'd yet to have needed one. He found this to be hard to believe but agreed to take it off and wear the headset anyway.

Todd handed them each rental headsets, and Lenny promptly removed his helmet and put the headset on right there in the lobby. The kid saw what his father was doing and followed suit.

"What do you think, Todd? Do they look ready to go?" I asked, hoping he would see these two standing in the middle of the lobby with their headsets already on and realize what a mistake this was.

"Yup, they look ready to me," he said, "You guys have a good flight."

What a jackass.

"Alright, let's head out to the plane," I told them.

Lenny followed me out the door onto the ramp with his son behind him. Both of them with their headsets on, the cords dragging on the ground behind them, carrying their army helmets under their arms.

Lenny Jr. was last through the door, and as it shut his mic cords caught the doorway and stripped his headset off his head knocking his mustache loose. We had to stop for a minute so Lenny could reapply it using a tube of glue he'd apparently been carrying in his pocket.

While this nonsense was going on, another instructor passed us on his way into the building. He paused for a moment when he saw Lenny reattaching his son's mustache, then gave me a look that asked, WTF?

I shrugged my shoulders and mouthed, *I don't know*.

As I got the plane ready to go, I explained to Lenny how it would go during the flight, as far as who was flying and when he would be allowed to touch the controls. This is something I did with everyone, but something told me that I should put extra emphasis on it today. It wasn't just that he seemed to be somewhat mentally unstable that concerned me; he was also twice my size. He was nearly 6' 5" and at least 250 pounds. If there were any confusion about who was going to be flying the plane, he was going to win the strength contest for sure. I had to make sure he understood, if I said, "My airplane," he needed to let go of the controls immediately.

"Yes, sir. I understand, instructor, sir! And, how many barrel rolls and loops will we be doing today, sir?"

"Ah, none today. This isn't really the right type of airplane for those kinds of maneuvers. Plus, that's a little advanced for someone who hasn't flown before. We're just going to be doing a little basic aircraft handling today. I'll teach you what each of the controls do; we'll practice holding the plane straight and level, make some turns. Things like that."

He started giggling, apparently thinking that was funny. I didn't really know how to take it, I but decided to press on.

"Alright, you ready?" I asked, as I hopped up onto the wing of the Warrior and opened the door.

He paused for a moment right behind the wing, looked down at the step, then asked, "Permission to come aboard, instructor, sir?"

"Permission granted," I told him, and off we went.

Lenny sat quietly with a blank stare straight ahead during the run-up and taxi out, but the moment we rotated, he grabbed the armrests and clenched tight. It was obvious pretty quickly that he was afraid.

"You OK, Lenny?"

"I'm scared, Mister," he responded, now speaking as if he were a child.

"It's alright; just relax," I told him.

Once we got up to 1,500 feet or so, I asked him if he wanted to take the controls a little. I figured the quicker I got him doing something and made him feel like he had a little control, he would hopefully calm down a little.

"Go ahead," I told him. "Just fly along with me."

He immediately grabbed the controls with a death grip. He was shaking so badly that I could not only feel it in the yoke, but I could feel the whole plane shaking.

"It's alright, Lenny," I told him. "Just use a light grip on the controls. We're going to make a left turn. I'm going to guide you through it."

"LEFT TURN, YES SIR, INSTRUCTOR SIR!" he shouted, snapping back into military mode.

I began applying pressure toward the left, but he was gripping the yoke so tightly on his side I was having to fight to overpower him.

The plane gradually began banking left, and when it did, he jerked the controls back toward the right.

"My airplane," I said, but he didn't let go.

"Lenny, let go for a second. My airplane."

"I want to go home now," he said. "I don't like this."

"That's fine, Lenny. We can go back, but I need you to let go of the controls, please. The tower is expecting us to turn left."

"I'm sorry, Mister."

He let go, and I immediately made a bank toward the left, but as soon as I did, he grabbed the yoke again. I fought him through the turn and called the tower, "Marbella Tower, five foxtrot alpha would like to make left traffic for a full stop."

"Five foxtrot alpha, make left traffic," the tower responded as I continued to fight him.

Once I completed the turn to downwind and we were back to straight and level flight, I told him, "Lenny, you've got to let go of the controls. I know you're scared, but I'm not going to be able to land us safely with you holding on like that."

"But I don't want to."

"Well, if you want to go home you have to."

He let go, and I told him to keep his hands down on his lap. For the moment he did, but I was afraid once we began descending and making turns toward the runway he was going to panic again.

At this point I was getting scared. This guy was unpredictable, his personality was changing by the minute, and he was in a serious state of panic right now.

I looked back over my shoulder to see Lenny Jr. with the fake mustache sitting peacefully in the backseat. He was seemingly unaware of what was going on, or maybe he was used to all this.

Abeam the numbers, I let him know that I was about to reduce the power and start descending. "Just keep your hands on your lap till we land," I said. "Don't touch anything."

"Yes, Mister." He responded, but as soon as I pulled the throttle back, he grabbed the controls again.

"Lenny, no! Let go!" I reached over with my left hand and pulled his hands off the yoke one at a time. He didn't fight me, but he immediately put them back.

As I turned to base, it continued and onto final. I kept telling him to let go, but he was no longer listening. I was flying with my right hand and using my left hand to both control the throttle and continually pull his hands off the yoke.

Several times I said, "My airplane, and, Lenny, let go," but his mood was changing from panic to goofing around like it was funny now.

By the time we were on short final, he was giggling like a toddler, and when I pulled his hand off the yoke, he said, "I'm going to touch it again."

"Man, this is not a game! Let go!" I shouted, but he didn't listen.

Then he jerked the controls around, and sounding like a complete psychopath, said, "I'm flying this airplane now, Mr. Instructor."

"No, you're not, Lenny. Let go; you're going to kill us."

As we crossed the threshold, I had to change my tactic to using both hands on the yoke, fighting to keep us under control. Trying to keep his hands off the controls wasn't working anymore.

It continued all the way to the flare and got to the point he was holding on so tight, it was taking everything I had to fight the plane onto the runway while overpowering him.

As soon as the mains hit, he freaked out and abruptly jerked the yoke to the right, kicking the right rudder pedal and brake in the process. We immediately veered off centerline, nearly rolled over, and were heading toward the grass. I quickly slammed on both brakes so hard I flat-spotted the mains down to the cords in a puff of black smoke. The plane came screeching to a halt just before running off the right side of the runway.

"Lenny, we're on the ground. Let go so we can taxi in. Everything's fine."

He snapped back into military mode, shouted, "Yes, sir, instructor sir!" and let go of the yoke.

The tower surprisingly didn't say anything to us about it. He just gave me taxi instructions to the ramp like nothing had happened. I guessed they were used to seeing student pilots nearly run off the runway down there; this was just an everyday occurrence for them.

When I parked the plane, we all got out. He and the kid both followed me into the building, still wearing their headsets with the cords dragging on the ground behind them.

"Todd will get you checked out," I told him once we were in the lobby. I didn't have anything else to say, and I don't think anything I would have said would have mattered anyway. The guy was a lunatic.

He and the kid both saluted me as I walked away toward the flight instructor's office.

I was shaken up from it. "That was the worst flight of my life," I told one of the other instructors, then proceeded to explain what had just happened. A few minutes into the story, Todd poked his head into the office.

"Looks like it went well," he said. "Lenny just signed up for the full course to get his private. He'll be back to fly with you again tomorrow."

I was in shock. "What, no! I'm not flying with him again. Put him on Ian's schedule."

"OK, if you don't want him. I'm sure Ian will take him."

"Yeah, Ian will love him. They'll be two peas in a pod. I think I need to go find George. I'm starting to miss him."

-14-
First Solo

The instructor crew was now on public transportation, which was a new low for us. We had been riding the bus to work since Dave left town with the Fleetwood.

Turns out we weren't the only broke pilots riding the bus to the airport, though. In fact, the whole bus was full of pilots. I guess none of us had a car. The guy sitting next to me that morning, who was in a pilot's uniform and slamming a bottle of vodka at 6:45 a.m., asked me if I knew of any jobs.

"Talk to Todd," I told him. "He'd probably hire you. He's looking for new instructors all the time, and it looks like you've already got a pretty solid system in place for coping with a shitty job."

"Alright, man, thanks. I'll call that Todd," he said as he took another swig of vodka.

Upon arriving at the flight school, I saw that George was back, and he was already outside, sitting in the plane waiting for me, but the fuel sump on the right wing of the Warrior was stuck wide open, and fuel was actively spilling out onto the ramp. He must have accidentally locked it open while he was sumping the tanks during the preflight and not noticed. The puddle that had already formed was at least five gallons and it was growing larger by the minute. I was about to run out and tell him, but Todd stopped me and said he needed to speak to me in his office.

"Ah, hang on a second," I told him. "I've got something I need to go take care of real quick."

But Todd insisted he speak to me immediately. "No, this can't wait," he said.

Well whatever, I thought, *I'm not the one paying for the fuel.* "Sure, I've got a few minutes," I said and followed him into his office.

"Shut the door," he told me.

I closed the door behind me and sat down.

"I need you to send George on his first solo."

"What? No way," I shot back. "I'm not signing him off to solo. He'll kill himself."

"Well, that's a risk we're going to have to take. He came in here this morning and told me that if he didn't get to solo soon, he was going to quit flying."

"Well, he should quit. He's got like 700 hours of instruction time now, and he still can't land a plane."

"No, we can't let him quit. He's one of the few students we have left. We can't afford to lose any more. The school is about to go under as it is. Do you want to be out of a job?"

"I'd rather be out of a job than lose my certificate sending someone solo who has no business being in an airplane in the first place. I'm not signing my life away."

"Come on, I'm sure he'll be fine. We've sent plenty of bad students solo before. What's one more?"

"George isn't just your average bad student. The guy barely survives each flight with me there helping him. If we let him go solo, he'll crash for sure and possibly kill others. No way! I'm not signing him off! He'll never make it! I mean, look out the window. He's sitting out there right now completely unaware that his right fuel tank is emptying onto the ramp."

Todd peered through the blinds. "Well, go tell him to shut that fuel sump, but I still need you to send him solo."

"No way."

"Fine then, I'll get someone else who will."

"If you do that, good luck."

"And maybe you should start looking for another job."

"Oh, trust me, I am."

Of course, Todd had no trouble finding another instructor to sign off George for a solo flight. His trusty sidekick Ian was more than willing to do it. But even for him, this was a new low. At this point, though, word was out that Ian had epilepsy. He had nothing to lose anymore. If this place went under, his days as a pilot would be over for sure, and with as many people who knew at this point, I couldn't believe the FAA hadn't shown up here to arrest him yet.

I went out to the ramp to talk to George. I let him know about the fuel spill, which at this point was going to require sand bags to contain and a hazmat crew to clean up, but mostly I was hoping I could convince him not to go solo even if Ian did sign him off. The time had come to be straight with him.

"You suck as pilot," I told him. "In fact, you're probably the most unqualified person to ever touch an airplane. I'm not going to sugar coat anything. If you go solo, you're probably going to die. Todd's going to get Ian to endorse you, but I'm begging you not to do it."

"I know I suck," George said. "But it's all I ever wanted to do. I just want to solo once, and then I'll be done with it. I swear. I'll throw away my bomber jacket and aviators and never come back here. I'll even throw away my *Top Gun* VHS tape. I just need to do it once, one landing. Otherwise, this was all for nothing."

"But in 700 hours you've never made one landing that wouldn't have been a crash had me or one of the other instructors not been there to save you. How are you going to do it on your own?"

"I promise, I'm going to use everything you taught me. I may not bring the plane back in one piece, but I think I can land good enough to walk away from it. It will be a good landing, I swear. It's all I ever wanted to do."

"I don't think it's a good idea, but you do what you've got to do. Todd's dead set on sending you so there's not much I can do to stop you. Just make sure you crash on the runway and don't hurt anyone else. And please don't buzz the tower. I'm serious; they'll arrest you, and you'll go to jail if you do."

Word spread through the flight school like wildfire that George was about to solo. Everyone gathered out on the ramp to witness his first and probably last solo flight and possibly his last moments on earth. When Ian endorsed his logbook, George held it high above his head for the entire crowd to see. He promptly climbed into the Warrior, and after about forty-five minutes of completing The King James Checklist, he was ready for departure.

He taxied out of his parking spot and across the ramp. Swinging wide through a turn, he scraped his right-wing tip across the nose cones of three other airplanes that were parked in a row as he headed for the taxiway, leaving a chunk of broken fiberglass and his right nav light behind.

Just as George got cleared for take-off, my phone rang. I looked at the caller ID; it was Dave. I ducked out of the crowd to answer the call.

"Hello," I answered.

"Hey Checkflight needs pilots bad; you need to apply here."

"I'm at 980.3 right now. I'm close but not quite there."

"They'll take you. Just call them."

"OK, I will. I've gotta go right now, but I will."

I looked up from the call just in time to see George rotate and pitch the Warrior near vertical. *Holy shit, this is going to end quick*, I thought.

The plane stalled, and the nose dropped, but he managed to break the stall just before hitting the ground and continued to climb out.

"WOO HOO! I feel the need . . . The need for speed!" he shouted over the tower frequency.

"Warrior five foxtrot alpha, make left traffic for two-three," the tower controller responded.

For a few minutes it was quiet as the crowd followed the Warrior through the traffic pattern. On downwind and abeam the numbers I saw his landing light switch on, then about twenty seconds later as he turned base it shut back off again, Then when he turned final, it turned back on again and stayed on this time. He must have done the King James before landing checklist three times. At least he ended on the right note with all the switches in the correct position.

He didn't seem to be slowing down, though. He looked fast and high on the glideslope.

When he reached short final, everyone held their breath as the Warrior came screaming down toward the runway. He was going way too fast.

"Deploy the arresting cable," he instructed the tower.

"Sir, we don't have an arresting cable here," the tower responded in an unbelievably monotone voice, considering the request.

He crossed the numbers and passed by in front of us. There was no flare at all. The nose wheel slammed into the runway, followed by the mains. The plane bounced airborne again. *Don't dump the flaps,* I thought as he slammed down nose first again, and then continued making bounce after bounce, again and again, porpoising down the runway with the prop striking the tarmac several times, each time throwing a shower of sparks in the air, till finally the Warrior settled down on all three wheels and rolled to a stop.

"Sir, are you OK?" the control tower asked George over the radio.

"Yes, I'm great!" George announced for all to hear, "I just made my first solo!"

The crowd erupted in applause.

"Congratulations," the controller said. "Make any left turn and taxi to the ramp."

Upon arriving on the ramp, it was clear the nose wheel on the Piper Warrior was completely crooked. The mangled prop pointed at a downward angle, most likely due to the engine mount separating from the firewall. As George made the turn into his parking spot a piece of the cowling fell off, exposing the right side of the engine. The plane rattled, squeaked, and shook, and as it came to a stop, the nose gear gave out completely. The nose slammed to the pavement, and the prop ground into the ramp, throwing chunks of concrete in every direction, till it came to a sudden halt.

Just then, a fire broke out from under the cowling, engulfing the entire front of the plane in flames. Thankfully, a ramp worker responded quickly to extinguish it.

Moments later, through the haze from the fire retardant, George jumped out onto the wing of the Warrior. In his aviators and bomber jacket, with his head held high, he threw his arms into the air and screamed, "I soloed!"

Everyone erupted in applause, and the crowd ran toward George to congratulate him. "Good job, George!" and, "You're a real pilot now!" People were screaming. George jumped off the wing of the Warrior into the arms of his new fans and crowd-surfed through the mob of people.

Other students were spraying him down with champagne, and confetti was flying through the air as he was passed around. It was a ridiculous celebration, and it went too far when one student, who had apparently been carrying, began firing a pistol into the air.

I waited around off to the side until things calmed down and George had finished signing autographs for all his new fans. Ian had forced himself into the middle of the excitement, trying to bask in the spotlight of being the instructor who had endorsed George for his first solo, and I wanted no part of it.

"Who wants a solo endorsement?" Ian shouted, and began randomly signing his CFI number in students' logbooks who were holding them up in the crowd. He must have endorsed twenty or thirty solo flights right then and there amidst the chaos. It was by far the stupidest thing I'd ever seen.

George finally emerged from the crowd and came toward me with the biggest smile I'd ever seen on his face.

"Congratulations on your first solo," I told him.

"I did good, huh?" George said.

I looked over at the plane, sitting there with its mangled nose gear, smashed up wing tip, and Q-Tipped prop. It looked like the engine was about to fall off and there was oil now running out of the bottom of the cowling toward the storm drain. *I guess it could have been much worse.* What really mattered was that George walked away from it without a scratch.

"Yup, you did good," I said.

"I want you to be the one to cut the back of my bomber jacket off," he told me. "Not Ian. You were my real instructor."

It had been a long-standing tradition in aviation that when a student made their first solo their instructor cut a square out of the back of their shirt. They wrote their name and the date on it and hung it up on the flight school wall along with every other students' shirt that ever made their first solo at that flight school. The student was supposed to wear the shirt with the back cut out of it for the rest of the day as a badge of honor for making their first solo flight.

But George wanted me to cut the back off his jacket?

"Are you sure you want me to ruin your good jacket?" I asked. "I mean, I'll cut your t-shirt instead; that's what we normally do."

"I'm sure," he told me. "This is the last time I'm going to wear it anyway. I made my first solo and that's all I ever wanted to do."

"Alright, let's do it."

George left that day with the back of his bomber jacket cut out, the proudest student I've ever seen leave this flight school. And while I was partially happy for him that his dreams came true here today, I still thought it was a ridiculously irresponsible thing for Todd and Ian to send him in the first place. After George was gone, I went to Todd's office to speak to him.

"I told you he'd do fine," Todd said to me.

"What's your definition of fine?" I asked. "That was a near disaster."

"Oh, it wasn't that bad."

"The plane is totaled!"

"That plane was old; it was insured. I been hoping someone would ding that thing up so I could collect on it anyway."

"You and your insurance money. If all you want is money for these planes, why don't you just sell them?"

"In this market?" Todd responded. "I wouldn't get much."

"Nice," I said. "Endanger lives to collect some insurance money."

"Hey, it's just business," he said as he kicked back in his chair and put his feet up on the desk. "Gotta do what I gotta do."

"Did you ever think of maybe running a legitimate business?"

"No, I never thought of that. I like my way better."

And right then I decided it was time. If Checkflight needed pilots bad, I was going for it. I hadn't even interviewed or even spoken to them yet, but I was definitely done here. I knew that much.

"Well, the reason I came in here," I said, "was to put my two weeks in."

"Oh, that won't be necessary, just get the fuck out now. You instructors with your two-week notices like you're some kind of professionals or something. I'll have you replaced by morning. There's the door."

"Fair enough," I said. "I'll see ya."

And that was it. I left.

My days as an instructor were over.

-15-
One Thousand Hours

I did get hired at Checkflight because, just like every other airline or flight school, they would take any sucker who was willing to do it. As long as you had a thousand hours in your logbook, could tell the gear was DOWN AND LOCKED, and were willing to fly a pile of garbage for nothing, you were in.

As for Todd's future, he carried on business as usual. I was easily replaceable. When me or any other instructor got fed up with it, there was a line of replacements waiting outside the door, all waiting to take their turn to earn their stripes with the hopes that one day there would be a light at the end of this tunnel and they would be respected as professionals like doctors and lawyers. Living the dream from their office in the sky.

Alex Stone

CFI! The Book

To find out what happens next read *Hauling Checks*.

Alex Stone

About the Author: Alex Stone grew up in Munster, Indiana. He's been flying since age fourteen and received a BS in aviation science from Western Michigan University. He has worked as a flight instructor and was a "Freight Dog" in the air cargo industry for seven years. In 2009 he published his first novel, *Hauling Checks*. *CFI! The Book* is his second novel.

Alex Stone

Glossary of Aviation Terms

Advisory Frequency: a frequency designated for the purpose of carrying out airport advisory practices while operating to or from an airport without an operating control tower.

AGL (Above Ground Level): a height measured with respect to the underlying ground surface, as opposed to altitude/elevation above mean sea level or (MSL).

Air Traffic Control (ATC): the ground-based personnel and equipment concerned with monitoring and controlling air traffic within a particular area.

Airworthiness Certificate: a certificate issued by the Federal Aviation Administration attesting that the aircraft named on the certificate has met all required design and performance criteria in force at the time of its manufacture.

Base: part of the traffic pattern, a flight path at right angles to the landing runway off its approach end. The base leg normally extends from the downwind leg to the intersection of the extended runway centerline.

Checklist: a list of tasks that should be performed by pilots and aircrew at a certain phase of flight.

Checkride: a practical test, more commonly known as a checkride, is the Federal Aviation Administration examination which one must undergo to receive an aircraft pilot's certification or an endorsement for additional flight privileges.

Downwind: part of the traffic pattern, a flight path parallel to the landing runway in the direction opposite to landing. The downwind leg normally extends between the crosswind leg and the base leg.

Federal Aviation Administration (FAA): a national US authority with powers to regulate all aspects of civil aviation.

Final approach: part of the traffic pattern, a flight path in the direction of landing along the extended runway centerline. The final approach normally extends from the base leg to the runway.

CFI! The Book

First Officer (FO): the second in command to the captain on an aircraft. Commonly known as the co-pilot.

Fixed Base Operator (FBO): an airport business that provides parking, flight training, aircraft maintenance and servicing, sales, charter service, and so on.

Flaps: surfaces added to the trailing and sometimes the leading edge of a wing. Actuation of the flap changes the curvature of the wing, increasing lift and drag, and allows an airplane to operate safely at lower speeds.

Flight Service: an FAA facility for relaying communications, furnishing weather and safety information to pilots, processing flight plans, and receiving VFR position reports.

Go Around (Missed Approach): a procedure followed by a pilot when a safe landing cannot be made or an instrument approach cannot be completed to a full-stop landing.

Ground Control: the position within a control tower organization responsible for the safe and expeditious movement of aircraft on the ground.

Heading Indicator: a gyroscopic navigation instrument used to give a more stable indication of an aircraft's heading than it is possible to achieve with a magnetic compass. It depends on other sources, such as a magnetic compass, for initial and updated directional alignment.

Hobbs Meter: a generic trademark for devices used in aviation to measure the time that an aircraft is in use.

Instrument Landing System (ILS): a precision runway approach aid based on two radio beams that together provide pilots with both vertical and horizontal guidance during an approach to land without visual references.

Instrument Rating: a rating added to a private pilot or commercial pilot license and refers to the qualifications that a pilot must have in order to fly under Instrument Flight Rules (IFR) and without visual references.

Magnetic Compass: a navigation instrument that displays a vehicle's orientation with respect to the magnetic poles by using the property of a bar magnet to align itself with the earth's magnetic force.

Mixture Control: a control in a reciprocating engine-powered aircraft that lets the pilot vary the fuel-air ratio or cut fuel to the engine completely.

Multi-Engine Rating: allows a pilot to operate as pilot-in-command of an aircraft with more than one engine.

Pattern: a standard path followed by aircraft when taking off or landing while maintaining visual contact with the airfield.

Pilot in Command (PIC): the pilot responsible for the operation and safety of an aircraft during flight time.

Private Pilot's License: a type of license that allows the holder to act as pilot in command of an aircraft privately (not for compensation).

Registration Certificate: a document issued by the FAA that shows the name and address of the owner of an aircraft, the manufacturer's serial number for the aircraft, and the register number it must display. It is analogous to the registration slip for an automobile.

VFR Sectional Aeronautical Chart: an aeronautical map intended for visual navigation of slow- and medium-speed aircraft under Visual Flight Rules (VFR).

Stall: the condition that exists when the angle of attack becomes so great that air no longer flows smoothly over an airfoil.

Visual Flight Rules (VFR): flight operating rules followed when weather is better than specified minimum cloud ceiling and visibility. In the United States, it is commonly used as synonymous to good weather.

Yoke: alternatively known as a control wheel, this device is used for piloting some fixed-wing aircraft.

www.cfithebook.com

Also by Alex Stone:

Hauling Checks

I'm a cargo pilot. In the industry, I'm known as a Freight Dog. I fly canceled checks and other types of high-value cargo around the country, mostly at night, in airplanes that are older than I am. Flying freight (or "work" as we call it) in small twin-engine aircraft is a lesser known side of the aviation world. Our day starts when bankers' hours end. Thousands of flights move millions of pounds of work from city to city every night, while the rest of the country is asleep. We're out there in the freezing rain getting de-iced when you're lying down for bed. We're sweeping the snow off our wings with a broom at three in the morning. That horrible thunderstorm you heard last night while you were sleeping: we were flying through it. The fog you woke up to in the early morning hours: we were landing in it.

Hauling Checks is a comedy about the darker side of aviation. A cast of degenerate pilots who work for a shady night-time air cargo operation take you on a flight through the unfriendly skies. The pilots abuse every reg in the book in their quest to make deadlines for their high-value cargo. As the company falls on hard times, management resorts to questionable measures to save the failing airline.

ISBN 13: 978-1449563332

Buy it on Amazon, ibooks, Barnes and Noble, or Smashwords

www.haulingchecks.com

Printed in Great Britain
by Amazon